Parables at Work

Parables at Work

John C. Purdy

The Westminster Press
Philadelphia

Book design by Christine Schueler

First edition

Published by The Westminster Press®
Philadelphia, Pennsylvania

PRINTED IN THE UNITED STATES OF AMERICA
9 8 7 6 5 4 3 2 1

Library of Congress Cataloging in Publication Data

Purdy, John C. (John Clifford), 1925–
    Parables at work.

    1. Jesus Christ—Parables. 2. Work (Theology)
I. Title.
BT375.2.P87 1985   233   84-17323
ISBN 0-664-24640-0 (pbk.)

Contents

Parables at Work

1
HOUSEKEEPING
The Parable
of the Leaven

To live well, we must learn to love well and to work well. Such was the teaching of Sigmund Freud of Vienna; thank you, Dr. Freud, for the valuable lesson. We Christians have learned from Jesus of Nazareth half of that lesson. Jesus has taught us how to love our neighbors and how to love ourselves. We have strategies for being loving to our spouses, parents, children, in-laws—even the grouch at the office. Should these strategies fail, we have at hand a clutch of therapies: pastors, counselors, radio call-in shows, self-help books, transactional analysis, encounter weekends, meditation. We also also have organized charities to channel love to brothers and sisters in Zaire, Pakistan, and Guatemala. We are experts in the art of loving.

Half of our homework is yet to be accomplished, however. We have yet to learn how to work well. We have no commonly accepted patterns of obedience for the workplace. Instead, we find ourselves bombarded by a stream of confused and confusing signals. Our young people hear that each of us has God-given talents; they also hear that the economy has few jobs to offer them. Adults hear that work is the best way to fill an eight-hour day—until they turn sixty-five, when they hear a rude "Sit down, old-timer!" As soon as she is old enough to hold a dolly, a girl might hear that she is to grow up to be a homemaker for the nourishment and nurture of children; when she is married and has those children, she may be told that if she wants them to have a good education, she must leave the house and join the work force. And what is her husband to think? He might have learned from his mother that a Christian woman's place is in the home; he may hear from his wife that she has God-given gifts that can be realized only in the business world.

Unscrambling such mixed signals is only part of the task demanded of Christians. We must also integrate two ways of defining ourselves. The church tells us that we are children of God and sisters and brothers of Jesus Christ, Sovereign of all life. Yet our society demands that we define ourselves in a different way. Society asks of each of us, "What do you do?" We dutifully reply: "I'm a lawyer," "I'm a housewife," "I'm a dental assistant," "I'm a steel-worker." Then society assures us that the answer we have given defines who we are.

In his travels down the back roads of America, described in *Blue Highways*, William Least Heat Moon tells of meeting a Tennessee farmer who also worked in a factory. "Factory work's easier on the back," the man told Moon, "and I don't mind it, understand, but a man becomes what he does. Got to watch that. That's why I keep at farmin', although the crops haven't ever throve. It's the doin' that's important." That farmer/factory hand understands how it is in our society: You become what you do. Your occupation defines you.

A mature Christian faith demands that we integrate the identity given us by the church and the one given us by our occupation. If we cannot integrate the two, we suffer an acute identity crisis. We wonder, What is a lawyer doing in the church? Or, conversely, What is a Christian doing in a law office? We may become like a friend of mine who in great frustration quit his job with a church publishing house. "I've tried to be a businessman among Christians," he told me. "Now I'm going to try being a Christian in the business world."

If there is a single reason why there are so many immature Christians in the pews, it lies at the juncture between faith and work. Faith that does not reach the "toiling core" of persons will never mean much to them. An established, commonly accepted pattern of Christian obedience for the workplace is one that enables persons to integrate faith and work. It enables them to fit together in harmony answers to the two questions: Who are you and What do you do? It is the assumption of this study that such a pattern is missing from our society.

No Work Ethic

Previous generations did not suffer such a lack. Our forebears had the Protestant work ethic, which decreed that each person's occupation in society was also his or her calling from God. Children of God showed obedience to their Heavenly Father by doing their absolute best in the workplace. Christian housewives cleaned cupboards to the glory of God; Christian students learned Latin to the glory of God; Christian merchants got rich to the glory of God.

In the centuries before the Protestant Reformation, there were two accepted ways of working oneself into heaven. Those who did not belong to religious orders did the tasks that their station in life dictated: Serfs tilled the soil; lords managed castles; merchants traded for goods; clerks scribbled—as clerks have done since the invention of writing. However, if one wanted to do one's work to the glory of God, it was necessary to join a religious order and become a nun, a priest, a monk. Inside the order, work suddenly became sacred: Nuns cooked to God's glory; monks tilled the monastery garden to God's glory; brothers copied manuscripts to God's glory. The work of serf and lord and merchant was secular; the work of nun and monk and priest was sacred. But no matter. The sacramental system of the church provided a sure way for serf and lord and merchant to work their way into heaven, just as Holy Orders did for nun and monk and priest.

In the earliest years of the church, many Christians were slaves or were lodged somewhere near the bottom of the social ladder. Roman society knew little and cared less about working to the glory of God. If the daily chores of the Christian slave did not interfere with the gathering of the church for worship on the first day of the week—and if this gathering did not incur the wrath of mistress or master—that was blessing enough. In such circumstances the Sunday liturgy—which in Greek means literally "the work"—was a sufficient opportunity to put faith to work.

None of these previous patterns will suffice for our generation. Our society is not so secular that we can be content to let Sunday worship be our only work to God's glory. Nor can we accept the notion that some occupations are holy and some secular. Even the vaunted Protestant ethic will not do for us; modern notions of work cannot fit that pattern, nor can the biblical witness be trimmed to fit it. We need new patterns of obedience for the workplace.

We need these as individuals, for our own integration
and maturity as Christians. We need them also for the
sake of the reign of God in the world. There is a danger-
ous trend in our society that we cannot allow to go un-
challenged: the increasing privatization of religion. More
and more, God is being shoved out of the public arena
and into the purely private spaces of life: the sanctuary,
the home, and the hour of meditation. Not to have ac-
ceptable patterns of obedience for the workplace is to
allow this trend to continue. Certainly, God will be
shoved out to the fringes of life if there is no place for
God in the workplace.

Therefore we shall attempt here the other half of that
homework assigned to us by Sigmund Freud. We shall
seek to learn from Jesus of Nazareth, our Teacher, what it
means to work well in his name and for his sake. We shall
seek to learn from Jesus patterns of obedience for the
workplace.

Jesus left us no direct teachings about faithfulness on
the job. What we have in the four Gospels are his teachings about the reign (kingdom) of God. About God's work
in and for the world. Mark tells us in his Gospel, "Now
after John was arrested, Jesus came into Galilee, preaching the gospel of God, and saying, 'The time is fulfilled,
and the kingdom of God is at hand; repent, and believe in
the gospel'" (Mark 1:14–15).

Jesus taught about the coming reign of God. He also
taught in parables—brief stories, vivid figures of speech.
Fortunately for the purpose of this study, many of Jesus'
parables were drawn from the workplace. "The kingdom
of heaven is like leaven which a woman took and hid in
three measures of flour" (Matt. 13:33). "For the kingdom
of heaven is like a householder who went out early in the

morning to hire laborers for his vineyard" (Matt. 20:1).
"The kingdom of God is as if a man should scatter seed
upon the ground" (Mark 4:26). Therefore we may hope
to find patterns of obedience in Jesus' teaching, even
though he left us no direct instruction about work. By
reflecting on his teaching about the better future that
God has for us, we may gain insight into what it might
mean for us to work faithfully in our present occupations.

Our process in this study will be in three steps; we shall
follow these three steps in each chapter. (1) We shall look
at one of Jesus' parables that is drawn from the world of
work, seeking to understand what this parable can teach
us about God's kingdom—God's present demand and better future. (2) Then we shall look at those aspects of work
that are reflected in the parable, seeking to deepen and
broaden our understanding of the workplace and what it
is that people do there. (3) Finally, and this is the most
delicate step in the operation, we shall put together the
insight from the parable and the insights from our work
experiences to see if we can then discern a pattern of
obedience. In the study of each parable, we shall hope for
that illuminating flash that is both the promise and the
reward of faithful Bible study.

In the Kitchen

Our study begins in that place where most of us first
became aware of the world of work—the kitchen. The
scene is familiar; a woman is preparing food for her family. "He told them another parable. 'The kingdom of heav-
en is like leaven which a woman took and hid in three
measures of flour, till it was all leavened'" (Matt. 13:33).
Few of us live in homes where bread is baked. But we can

use our imaginations. A breadmaker puts a pinch of yeast into a much greater amount of flour. Once the yeast has permeated the flour, the leavened loaf is baked into bread.

The kingdom of God's righteousness works in a way similar to that yeast, Jesus wants us to know. There is a steady, slow, but pervasive penetration of the present by God's future. In, with, and under the unjust structures of this world, divine justice is at work.

It is tempting to draw from the parable an additional teaching about the hidden nature of God's work among us. But we shall stick to the consideration of one central point made by the parable—that the kingdom has the power to pervade.

There are sound reasons for limiting our interpretation of a parable. Parables are comparisons. Jesus described one reality by likening it to another. He took tangible entities, such as leaven and seeds and householders, and told us that an unseen reality—the kingdom of God—was in some way like them. We may suppose that Jesus chose to describe the kingdom by comparing it to yeast because one single feature of leaven attracted his attention. That is how comparisons work; we see in one thing a striking similarity to a major aspect of another. So we are most likely to remain faithful to Jesus' intent if we limit ourselves to one main point in each of his parables.

That means we must avoid the temptation to allegorize—to look for meaning in each detail of the parable. That leads into swamps of fantasy and speculation. Look, for example, at what can happen when we allow the Parable of the Leaven to be allegorized. Some interpreters would say that the flour is the world, the leaven is the church, and the time it takes for the leaven to work itself through the flour is the time allotted to human history. No, say others. The measures of flour are the church, the leaven is the gospel, and God is patiently waiting for the gospel to be believed by the whole church; then the end will come.

But look at the parable. Jesus did not say that God is like a housewife, or that the church is like flour, or that the gospel works like yeast. He made none of those comparisons. He said that the kingdom of heaven is like a small amount of leaven that pervades a large amount of flour. Or, as we have interpreted the likeness, the better future God has for us is already invading and permeating the structures of this present world.

Domestic Chores

Let us back off from that point to consider the nature of the workplace as it is reflected in the parable. The story shows us a woman going about the task of preparing food for her family. That view of the workplace is all too familiar; it is the place of domestic chores. Every job, with scarcely an exception, consists mostly of chores. One of the bedrock, bone-wearying, unyielding characteristics of work is that it thrusts us into domestic routine.

Most of us, much of the time, are busily engaged in some sort of domestic chore. For many, these are tasks that keep a household running: washing, preparing food, cleaning, dusting, ironing, sewing, gardening. For those in schools, the tasks are those that keep the academic household going: attending classes, giving lectures, hearing lectures, taking notes, taking exams, grading exams. And for how many of us is office work largely a matter of domestic routine? Typing, filing, phoning, going to meetings: Office workers even refer to these as "housekeeping chores." Likewise, in a factory or foundry there are the tasks of caring for tools, sweeping floors, filling out forms—the whole deadly array of keeping things tidy.

It is no accident that the word "economy," which serves as an umbrella term for our combined work, is derived from a Greek word meaning "household." One of the essential features of what this study means by *work* is that it involves us in domestic routine.

Why else this love/hate thing we have with work? We crave the structure that work gives our lives, even as we resist the boredom. Office workers grumble about the meetings they must attend; they grumble just as loudly if meetings are never called. The worker who retires from the factory sets out at once to build a routine to take the place of the assembly line.

Until God's better future is realized, work will have for all of us something of the nature of domestic routine. The woman in Jesus' parable, leavening flour to prepare bread for her family, is a fair representative of each of us in our places of work.

What Pattern?

Now let us feed that insight back to the main point of the parable, that the better future even now pervades the structures of the present. What pattern of obedience for daily work is suggested? The answer may be phrased as follows: *When we cannot escape the necessity of chores, we may do them cheerfully and patiently, knowing that in, with, and under such labor the better future is already at work.*

We have been programmed to mistrust statements like that. It sounds a bit too much like "Everyone's job is a calling from God." We have determined that such an ethic is not suitable for us. So let us restate the insight in the negative: *There is no way into the better future that detours around the drudgery of domestic chores.*

That is not to say that all who do housework are serving God. George MacLeod, founder of a religious community at Iona, Scotland, would occasionally volunteer to scrub the toilets. "So I won't be tempted to preach sermons on the nobility of work," he explained. Heaven help us if we perverted our scriptural insight into a romanticizing of housework. Within the living memory of many, housework has proved anything but romantic. In *Growing Up*, Russell Baker recalls what life was like for his mother and grandmother in Virginia in the late 1920s:

> Both my mother and grandmother kept house very much as women did before the Civil War. . . . Their lives were hard, endless, dirty labor. They had no electricity, gas, plumbing, or central heating. No refrigerator, no radio, no telephone, no automatic laundry, no vacuum cleaner. Lacking indoor toilets, they had to empty, scour, fumigate each morning the noisome slop jars which sat in bedrooms during the night.
>
> For baths, laundry, and dishwashing, they hauled buckets of water from a spring at the foot of a hill. To heat it, they chopped kindling to fire their woodstoves. They boiled laundry in tubs, scrubbed it on washboards until knuckles were raw, and wrung it out by hand. Ironing was a business of lifting heavy metal weights heated on the stove top.

They scrubbed floors on hands and knees, thrashed rugs with carpet beaters, killed and plucked their own chickens, baked bread and pastries, grew and canned their own vegetables, patched the family's clothing on treadle-operated sewing machines, deloused the chicken coops, preserved fruits, picked potato bugs and tomato worms to protect their garden crop, darned stockings, made jelly and relishes, rose before the men to start the stove for breakfast and pack lunch pails, polished the chimneys of kerosene lamps, and even found time to tend the geraniums, hollyhocks, nasturtiums, dahlias, and peonies that grew around every house. By the end of a summer day a Morrisonville woman had toiled like a serf.

No, there is nothing romantic about housekeeping! Nevertheless, the inescapable, sometimes maddening weight of domestic routine is lightened immeasurably by the confidence that somehow concealed in it the kingdom of God may be at work.

When I was a small boy in Ohio, my widowed mother was our breadwinner; she worked outside the home. My widowed grandmother was the breadmaker; she kept house for the four of us and did most of the chores. Although she had raised six children of her own, Grandma took on the cooking, cleaning, and ironing for our family. She did it with a cheerfulness that to me is still a marvel. After all these years I can still remember the smile with which she tackled the toughest job—and the quaint sayings that she used to lighten chores. "Don't just give it a lick and a promise," she would say. Or, "That needs a bit of elbow grease."

I thought Grandma had a very limited worldview. She had not gone to college; she did not know the batting order of the Cleveland Indians; she insisted that in all the world there could not be a sight more lovely than an Ohio farm. There must be billions of workers in the world today whose universe is as limited as was Grandma's. Yet, if we have correctly understood the Parable of the Leaven, such workers are not far from the kingdom of God.

The woman in Jesus' parable and persons like my grandmother may serve as models for the Christian worker. Does that surprise you? Does it greatly disappoint you? Did you expect something more grand, more exciting, than *housekeeping* as a pattern for faithful service to God? Then you know too much about the past and the present and too little of the future. "For the kingdom of heaven is like leaven which a woman took and hid in three measures of flour, till it was all leavened."

2
REWARDS
The Parable
of the Hidden Treasure

The world asks a serious question—Who will inherit the better future?—to which the kingdom parables of Jesus offer what seems a whimsical answer. The question is asked in a variety of ways: Will it be the poor and the oppressed? Or will it be the technological elites? Will it be the workers of the world, who have borne the burden and heat of the day? Or will there be a share for the idle rich? Does God lean to the side of the Western democracies or to the side of the socialist countries of the Second World? But in all these various questions the bottom line is this: Who has a right to the rewards?

To such questions the Bible replies only: The kingdom appears as a joyful surprise. Jesus said, "The kingdom of heaven is like treasure hidden in a field, which a man found and covered up; then in his joy he goes and sells all that he has and buys that field" (Matt. 13:44). The better future promised by God discloses itself unexpectedly, bringing great delight. Such is the teaching of the Parable of the Hidden Treasure.

In this series we are following the rule that each parable makes a single point. In the case of the Parable of the Hidden Treasure, that point is: Whenever humankind is rewarded with a glimpse of the divine reign of peace and justice, that appearance is both unexpected and delightful.

This should astonish no one who knows the Bible. For the history of God's appearances to humankind is a succession of joyful surprises. When humans were created—so the book of Genesis tells us—there was at first a sole being with no companions save the animals. God saw that the human being was lonely. So God took a rib from the human and fashioned woman and brought her to man. The first man could not have been presented with anything more surprising and better designed for delight. The narrator of the Genesis account (2:23) tells us that the man broke into poetry:

> This at last is bone of my bones
>   and flesh of my flesh;
> she shall be called Woman,
>   because she was taken out of Man.

And to this present day, poets testify that in sexual encounters there is always the possibility of joyful surprise.

Later in the book of Genesis, Sarah and Abraham are chosen by God as the couple whose seed will generate a Chosen People. There is just one hitch, however: Both are quite old, and Sarah is well past the menopause. When messengers from God appear and declare that a child will indeed be born to her, Sarah is seized with bitter laughter. But certainly Sarah has the last laugh, a cry of joyful surprise, when Isaac is born to her in her old age. The name Isaac means "he laughs," a way of declaring him to be God's joyful surprise.

Being God's Chosen did not prevent the Hebrews from being driven by famine to Egypt and there being enslaved by the Pharaohs. But Moses led them out to freedom, aided by God's blowing aside the waters of the sea to allow their escape. And when the Hebrews looked behind them and saw that the waters had rolled back and destroyed their enemies, the women—led by Miriam—seized tambourines and danced in wild delight.

After forty years of wandering in the wilderness that lay between Egypt and the promised homeland, the Hebrews came to Canaan; they found it defended by a walled city. At God's command, they marched mutely around the city for six days, while their priests blew trumpets. But on the seventh day, when the trumpets sounded once more, the people gave a great shout and the walls of Jericho fell down! The city and the land were theirs. Now that was a happy surprise!

And what of the shepherds in the hills outside Bethlehem, more than a millennium later? They were citizens of the remnant kingdom of Judea, a mean little lump of the Roman Empire. One night, out of a dark sky came a flash of light and this sudden announcement: "Be not afraid; for behold, I bring you good news of a great joy which will come to all the people; for to you is born this day in the city of David a Savior, who is Christ the Lord" (Luke 2:10–11).

The technical names for appearances of God are "theophanies" and "epiphanies." Whenever they happen in the scriptural account, which is infrequently, they are like bolts of sunshine piercing the blues. But they are neither arbitrary nor whimsical; they are continuing episodes in a larger story. The Bible does not portray God as Santa Claus, who drops by once in a while with good gifts for some and not for others. Nevertheless, who is closest to the kingdom of God? Is it the grim-jawed revolutionary,

who sees in every historical event the working out of a
divine plan to remake the world according to some ideology? Is it the flap-jawed fanatic, who reads the future in
signs and stars and numbers and thinks to discern exactly
how and when God's future will unroll? Or is it rather
that child who just once on Christmas has been gloriously
surprised by a gift beyond his or her wildest expectations?
The Parable of the Hidden Treasure points to the child.

The insight that God's reign appears as a glorious surprise comes to musical expression in the second movement of Brahms's *German Requiem*. There is a long and
solemn statement by the chorus, which many would regard as an accurate summation of all that we know about
the human condition:

> Behold, all flesh is as the grass,
> and all the goodliness of man is as the flower of
>   grass.
> For lo, the grass withereth,
> and the flower thereof decayeth.

(Brahms took that statement from 1 Peter 1:24, which is
in turn a free translation of Isaiah 40:6–7.)
After this statement there is a pause; then the chorus,
with a change in key, declares in full voice:

> Albeit, the Lord's word endureth forever more.
> The redeemed of the Lord shall return again,
> and come rejoicing, unto Zion;
> gladness, joy everlasting, joy upon their heads
>   shall be;
> joy and gladness, these shall be their portion;
> and tears and sighing shall flee from them.

While the chorus is making this declaration (based on Isaiah 35:10), there rises above the choir and the orchestra the exultant shout of a trumpet. It seems to echo the blast when the walls of Jericho tumbled; it is like the trumpet that called the Hebrews to Sinai to receive the law; it anticipates the final trumpet that shall wake the dead on the day of resurrection.

Throughout all of Scripture, sounding a note as defiant and joyous and unexpected as that trumpet, is the news of God's appearing. It does not happen according to timetable or ideology. Rather, it is God's joyful surprise. That is the one point to which we must hold firm in our consideration of the Parable of the Hidden Treasure.

Hired Hands

In each of these chapters we seek not only the central teaching of a parable; we want also to consider what that parable implies about the nature of work. What is there in the Parable of the Hidden Treasure that mirrors the workplace as we daily experience it?

The scene is a field. Since the man uncovers the treasure in that field, we may suppose that he is hoeing or plowing. As he does this menial task, he accidentally uncovers something of great value. Presumably it was buried there long ago for safekeeping —and forgotten. Since the man goes off at once to sell everything he owns to possess that field, we infer that the field is not his. He is a day laborer, a hired hand, a tenant farmer working for another and hence not the possessor of much of this world's goods. For it takes all that he owns to buy the land.

Who better than a hired hand to represent us in our work? At the end of the nineteenth century, in a fervor of sympathy for the workers of the world, the poet Edwin Markham sought a symbol for those toilers. He found it in Millet's painting of a French peasant. And Markham wrote "The Man with the Hoe." It begins:

> Bowed by the weight of centuries he leans
> Upon his hoe and gazes at the ground,
> The emptiness of ages in his face,
> And on his back the burden of the world.

Who of us, in some way, cannot empathize with that bent figure? We all tithe the products of our sweat and tears to "someone" who runs the company or owns the business or calls the shots. We get cash for our labor, but someone else usually gets the credit. Few of us have the satisfaction of owning the fruits of our work. We do not get the full reward due us; someone profits from our toil.

We can sympathize with the waitress in Studs Terkel's *Working:*

> The more popular you are, the more the boss holds it over your head. You're bringing them business, but he knows you're getting good tips and you won't leave. You have to worry not to overplay it, because the boss becomes resentful and he uses this as a club over your head. . . . It's not the customers, never the customers. It's injustice.

The next time you are on a coffee break or a lunch hour with fellow employees, listen to how often "they" creeps

into the conversation—"they" being the bosses, the owners, the managers who run the show, who get the glory
and the gravy while the rest do the nitty and the gritty.
Not many people work for themselves and themselves
alone. The so-called "workers' revolution" in Russia did
not produce a classless society, in which all might call
their labor their own. Those who work the mines, the
fields, and the factories still scramble under the lash of
quotas—imposed so that "they" can buy at "their" special
shops and drive "their" limousines to "their" summer
homes. And here in the land of the free and the home of
the brave, the house of the freest and bravest is taxed—in
part—so that those who set the tax rates can live at a level
of luxury well above that of the average worker.

The point need not be hammered home until the wood
splits! Nevertheless, we know about hired hands. We can
recognize the man in Jesus' parable, toiling in a field to
raise crops that will not be entirely his own. He could be
any one of us; all of us are, to some degree, hired hands.
What we call our *work* has something of the character of
that which is done in someone else's field for someone
else's profit.

But enough of that. What about the pattern of obedience? What can we learn from the Parable of the Hidden
Treasure about faithfulness to Jesus Christ in our places
of work? Remember, in our study of the parables we are
committed to a three-step movement, not unlike the
three steps in a waltz. We move forward by first stepping
a bit to one side. Well, we have taken the initial steps. We
have distilled from the parable a single truth about God's
kingdom, that it appears as a joyful surprise. And we have
let ourselves be reminded that we are all hired hands,
working in fields belonging to others. Now we are ready

for the third and final step, in which we attempt to discern a pattern of obedience for the Christian worker.

Three Temptations

But this final step is not an easy one. To complete it, we
must dodge three temptations. These arise from our encounter with the parable itself. The first is the temptation
to pay undue heed to those feelings of self-pity that arise
when we are reminded that we are all hired hands. There
is a little inner voice that whispers insistently, "Don't
worry. You'll get yours. Hard work and sacrifice pay off in
the end." True, in the parable the treasure is not discovered by a banker in the cool of a vault, or by a landlord
sitting in the shade, or by a foreman watching hired hands
sweat under a hot sun. It is found by one who bears the
heat and burden of the day. How near at hand, then, it
lies to recite the virtues of hard work, to recall the fable
of the ant and the grasshopper, and to adduce such sayings as "Pray as though all depended upon God; work as
though all depended upon you."

But thank God that the Parable of the Hidden Treasure
does not say or even imply that the kingdom will appear
only if we bend our wills and break our backs. Rather, it
says that the reign of God appears as a joyful surprise.

And now for the second temptation—more subtle,
more plausible than the first. This is the temptation to
submit to the demand of the liberationists. They insist
that the kingdom appears only to peasants and peons, to
those who work for Third World oligarchs. It is hard for
those who know the Scriptures not to yield to this demand. For did not Jesus himself say, "Blessed are you
poor, for yours is the kingdom of God" (Luke 6:20)? But

we do well to remember that in his own temptations, Jesus had to cope with one who quoted Scripture. We must not make of the Parable of the Hidden Treasure something that Jesus did not intend. We must hold fast to our insight about the kingdom appearing as a joyful surprise.

But what and where does that leave us? Just at this point: *Even as we work as hired hands in fields belonging to others, we may hope for the appearance of the reign of God.* We are not doomed to sullen acceptance of work tithed and taxed for the profits of others. We have a choice; we may be of good cheer. Like the treasure hidden in the field, the rule of God's peace and justice is concealed in the very midst of the places where we do our work. We may whistle while we work without being guilty of chirpy optimism. We may choose to be the liberated ones. Although we may never be free in the sense that we labor only at what we enjoy and only for what is best for ourselves, nevertheless we may be emancipated from the sullen, hopeless role of the indentured servant. For we know of something hidden from the rich, the proud, the absentee landlords and landladies. We know that hidden in those very fields they regard as theirs is a great treasure. We do not as yet possess it; yet the knowledge of it may possess us. And it may suddenly and joyfully appear.

It is just here that the third and most subtle of the three temptations now attacks us. Knowing that the kingdom is so near at hand, we may be tempted to go and sell everything we have so that we—in this very hour—may possess it. Like the laborer in Jesus' parable, we may want to rush off and dispossess ourselves in the hope of possessing God's kingdom. It is told of Francis of Assisi that when he

decided to cease being rich and spoiled and instead to
follow Christ, he stopped a beggar in the street and gave
him the clothes from off his body!

There are Scriptures that we might quote to justify
such a move. Jesus said to a rich young man, "If you
would be perfect, go, sell what you possess and give to
the poor, and you will have treasure in heaven; and come,
follow me" (Matt. 19:21). But in his Parable of the Hidden Treasure, Jesus tells of the man's selling all his possessions only to underscore the supreme joy of discovery.
The parable is not a summons to you and me to do likewise. Like hounds that drop the trail of a fox to tree a
possum, we would then be diverted from the main teaching of the parable. Its central point is that the kingdom
appears as a joyful surprise. We must not be diverted
from that teaching.

Work the Fields

The pattern of obedience suggested by the Parable of
the Hidden Treasure is not to sell everything, like Francis
of Assisi, or to throw ourselves into movements for the
liberation of the oppressed of the Third World, or even to
work harder in the fields to which we have been assigned.
*It is to work in our assigned fields in cheerful anticipation
of that day when our reward may suddenly appear.*

One summer I wrote a public relations story about a
church hunger project in New Mexico. The project was
run by two hired hands, Becky and David. They had
signed on for two years at subsistence wages. Dave had
trained as an anthropologist; Becky's specialty was Fine
Arts. Their assignment was to work five acres of irrigated
desert land. They spent a minimum of twelve hours a day,

under a scorching sun, hoeing vegetables, tending goats, and fighting Russian knapweed. What they hoped to discover in their field was an appropriate technology for the marginal farms of Rio Arriba County, one of the poorest in the entire United States. When I met with them, about all they had to show for their labor was a grand crop of blisters. But they were as hopeful and cheerful a pair of hired hands as I have ever met.

To whom does the future belong? Surely, if to anyone, then to the Beckys and Davids of this world. It belongs to all who believe—against all evidence—that in the fields of this world, however parched and merciless, there is concealed a kingdom of peace and justice for all.

3
EXCELLENCE
The Parable of the Pearl Merchant

It might do us good to read the Bible while standing on our heads. We might better appreciate how often Scripture inverts our normal way of seeing things. For example, we usually perceive the present as determined by the past. What exists, we say, is the outgrowth of what once was. As the child is mother to the woman, so today was shaped by yesterday. Therefore we help children to understand their civilization by teaching them history. We report to them significant events in their past, especially great discoveries. They learn about the discovery of America by Christopher Columbus, the invention of the steamboat by Robert Fulton, the discovery of radium by Marie Curie. These all stand like milestones, marking both whence and how far humankind has come.

Jesus taught a different way of looking at the world. Human affairs, he taught, are ultimately ruled by what has yet to be discovered. If you would know the realm of God, imagine a treasure hunt. "The kingdom of heaven," Jesus said, "is like a merchant in search of fine pearls, who, on finding one pearl of great value, went and sold all that he had and bought it" (Matt. 13:45–46).

The Parable of the Pearl Merchant makes the point that the reign of God is a relentless search for excellence. As the North Pole acts like a giant magnet, drawing all compass needles in its direction, so the prize set by God at the end of history orients human affairs. The book of Revelation describes the Holy City—symbol of God's better future—as built of precious metals and jewels; its streets are paved with gold, its gates are made of pearl. That is a fabulous way of telling us that up ahead, as yet unrevealed, lies the greatest treasure.

The Greeks had a different idea. Some of their philosophers taught that goodness, beauty, and truth are eternal. There was beauty in the past; there is truth today; there will be goodness in the future, they said. But the Bible has a different understanding of values. Would you know what God prizes the most? Then look to the future. The best and the truest and the most beautiful are yet to be disclosed to humankind. They are like the pearl of great price, which the merchant, in his search, has yet to find.

That insight stands conventional wisdom on its head. You may be a deist, who believes that God wound up Creation like a great clock and set it going. You may be a Darwinist, who believes that the hinge of history is that evolutionary moment when *Homo sapiens* developed a marvelously adaptive brain. Or you may be a creationist, who believes that in the beginning God created the world in six calendar days. But no matter where on that spectrum of belief you locate yourself, like most moderns you probably accept the "rowboat" notion of history: We can tell where we are and can judge where we are headed by looking back to where we have come from.

But what if Jesus, in his Parable of the Pearl Merchant, has charted an accurate course for history? What if, indeed, the kingdom of God is like the search for that which is of great value? Then that which is as yet to be discovered is what determines the course of events. History is not so much humankind's flight from savagery as it is a race for a grand prize. The end of things is not the natural outcome of what was in the beginning, as a tree is the natural outgrowth of a seed. Rather, the end of all things is like the golden trophy at the end of a race—a prize of such worth that it lures all runners, erasing from their minds the sound of the starting gun and making momentary and unimportant the pains in legs and chest. Thus the apostle Paul could write, "But one thing I do, forgetting what lies behind and straining forward to what lies ahead, I press on toward the goal for the prize of the upward call of God in Christ Jesus" (Phil. 3:13–14).

Testing the Chosen

Why else does Scripture record such relentless testing of those whom God chooses? If God elects persons because of their intrinsic merit, why do they need to be proved and tested, like pearls ground between the teeth of a prospective buyer? From the Bible's description of the constant, sometimes ruthless probing of God's Chosen, we get the impression that God examines each person who is chosen to see if he or she is worthy of the purposes God has in view.

In Genesis 22 is the narrative of Abraham and Isaac. It stands as prologue to the story of God's dealing with the Chosen Ones. The story begins: "After these things God tested Abraham . . ." (Gen. 22:1). Abraham, who is called to be the ancestor of all the blessed of God, has been given one son. And now God "puts the bite" on Abraham, to see if he is of such loyal stuff as patriarchs are made of.

God asks the ultimate sacrifice—the life of Abraham's only son. Abraham is equal to the test. He takes Isaac to the mountain, builds an altar, lays the wood for a fire, binds his son, lays him upon the wood, and raises a knife to do what God has commanded. At the critical moment God intervenes and stops the test; Abraham has passed; he is worthy of the purposes for which God intends him.

The people of Israel, who called Abraham their father and believed themselves chosen by God through him, were to relive over and over that same experience of being tested by God. Every time Israel came to believe that "chosen" meant the equivalent of "meritorious," times got tough. They discovered the hard way that they had been chosen, not because of merit but because of the great prize God hoped to win through them for all humankind.

One of the books of the Old Testament that was written later is Job. It could well stand at the very end of the Old Testament, for it reads like an epilogue to the story of God's dealings with Israel. It is the poetic saga of a man who is in every way God-fearing. But Satan is allowed by God to test Job, to see if Job fears God only because he has all that a man could want and desire. And so every sorrow and difficulty known to humankind are visited upon Job: the death of loved ones, the loss of goods, sickness, mental anguish. Job has great difficulty in believing that a gracious God would allow all this to happen to one who had done God no wrong. Even so did Israel, through its long history with God, wonder aloud:

> My God, my God, why hast thou forsaken me?
> Why art thou so far from helping me, from the
> words of my groaning?

O my God, I cry by day, but thou dost not answer;
and by night, but find no rest.

(Psalm 22:1–2)

Both Job and Israel must have felt, in their hours of testing, like the elderly saint who complained of her troubles
to her pastor. He assured her that God was merely testing
her. To which she replied with a weary sigh, "Sometimes
I wish the Lord did not have such a high opinion of me."

Even Jesus, declared from heaven to be God's beloved,
did not escape testing. We read in the Gospels that as
Satan was allowed to test Job, so Satan was allowed to put
Jesus to the test. It was following the baptism of Jesus by
John in the River Jordan. After the voice from heaven had
declared the newly baptized Jesus to be God's beloved,
Jesus was led by the Spirit into the wilderness to be
tempted. And all three temptations took essentially the
same form: If you are indeed chosen and beloved of God,
said Satan, then God will do whatever you want. Test God
to see if you are indeed the Chosen One: Turn stones into
bread. Throw yourself off the temple roof. Accept from
me the rulership of all the kingdoms of earth.

What else can explain this relentless probing of God's
cherished ones except that God was proving them to see
if they were worthy of the divine purpose? What else can
explain such endless testing but that the kingdom of God
is like a merchant in search of fine pearls, who probes and
examines each pearl—searching always for the best?
What is history, as the Bible reveals it, but God's relentless search for excellence?

But enough about searching. What about *finding?* For
the Parable of the Pearl Merchant tells of the discovery of
a pearl of great value. More than that, the pearl is of such

excellence that the merchant sells everything else in order to possess it. Surely the point of the parable is the search—not the final discovery. Yet the inclusion of the purchase of the one pearl reminds us of another dimension of the reign of God. We are not to suppose that the prize set at the end of history is like a pot at the end of a rainbow, whose value is unknown. Though the prize has yet to be uncovered, its value has been set. God paid with the life of the Beloved Child. "For God so loved the world that he gave his only Son . . ." (John 3:16).

The Search for Excellence

The metaphor of the pearl merchant is biblical history in a nutshell; it also serves as a mirror image of the workplace. Work is also marked by a relentless search for excellence. The workplace is a marketplace where people and things are continually being tested for value. Whatever else we mean by the term "work," we would want to include in any complete definition the never-ending search for excellence.

Another way of saying the same thing is to declare that work is value-determined. That is one of the primary characteristics distinguishing human work from the efforts expended by animals or machines. The work that a monkey does in gathering fruit is qualitatively different from the farmer's labor of planting an apple tree, grafting, pruning, and, at harvesttime, gathering the apples. There is no value at stake in the monkey's daily collecting of fruit, except, perhaps, the value of survival. But it does matter how the farmer plans and prunes and pollinates. There was a time when humans were, like monkeys, gatherers. But eventually, settled agriculture replaced gathering as a means of providing for physical wants. And there is no way humans can return to an economy of gathering fruits and nuts without regressing to a less human state. Settled agriculture is not only more efficient as a survival technique, it is a *better* way of securing food.

Work is value-marked and value-determined. In the long run, good work overcomes bad work; excellent work drives out the merely good. That was one of the findings of the authors of *In Search of Excellence,* the best-selling book on corporate management of the early 1980s. Thomas J. Peters and Robert H. Waterman found one of the secrets of successful companies to be that their leaders were conveyors of strong values. Not only did the more excellent corporations make a profit, they provided meaning for their employees. They were highly value-oriented. They were ruled by such notions as service, dependability, quality.

There was a time when economists spoke of "an invisible hand" that guided the world of work. This hand, they claimed, directed the economies of the world. It was usually described as self-interest—each person pursuing what was best for him or her. If this hand was allowed to operate unchecked—free from governmental interference—things would work out for everyone for the best.

The economists were half right. There is an invisible hand that governs the economies of the world. But it is not the law of self-interest, nor is it the law of supply and demand. Rather, it is the rule of excellence. Every kind of labor that goes into making up an economic system, whether that system be communism or capitalism, is finally governed by a standard of excellence inherent in that work. Any system that persistently ignores that standard will, in the long run, not survive.

That standard, however, is fully known only to those who are inside a particular field of endeavor. Only a merchant of pearls can recognize the pearl of supreme value. To those outside the field, a cultured pearl is scarcely distinguishable from one created by an oyster in the wild state. And to the untutored eye, a necklace of dime-store pearls may be as attractive as the real thing. But the merchant of pearls knows the difference at a glance.

Of the craft of writing, Mark Twain once observed, "The difference between the right word and the almost right word is the difference between lightning and the lightning bug." To those who only read what others have written, words may be just sounds reduced to symbols and put down on paper. But to those who write for a living, there is a great gulf between mere words on a page and fine writing. And so it is with every craft.

During World War II, I worked one summer in a rolling mill, where high-speed steel was manufactured. Some of that steel, we were told, went to make parts for military aircraft. For my first few weeks on the job, all work was a stew of noise, heat, and exhaustion. I took an instant liking to old Shell Morgan, who bossed our crew of helpers; I feared and hated Swede Lundberg, who bossed the crew of the ten-inch mill. Swede had lost a hand to the rollers, and with it whatever kindness he may once have had. But by the end of the summer, I had no doubt as to which of those two bosses was the excellent worker and which would be let go when the war was over and the demand for steel suddenly reduced. I would not have hesitated to go up in a fighter plane made from the steel that passed through Swede's hands; I wouldn't trust boozy old Shell to make the blade of a pocketknife! There is good work and there is bad work. And anyone who works very long inside a factory or office or store knows which is which.

The negative way of saying this is to say that work is never "value-free." There is no work that is good in itself, that does not serve some useful or valued end. Parents learn this when they try to foist off make-work on their children, supposing that work is good for growing bodies, even if it has to be invented. Children are not fooled by work that is trumped up to keep them busy or to teach them good habits. They know that work is value-laden. Many children will willingly do even hard work if the task has some value attached to it—such as money or praise or prizes. But they can smell make-work all the way across the front yard. And a kid with any sense will run away from it!

We would be more aware of the rule of excellence that governs all work if the artist, rather than the athlete, were the more common model of the worker. Our culture is so sports-conscious that we tend to draw our metaphors for work from sports. We talk of "winners and losers," of "champions," of "scoring a home run," of "coming in first." Even the apostle Paul, as we have seen, could speak of life as a footrace! And there was a time when it was the excellence inherent in sport that made it a mine of ready metaphors for daily work. There is an intrinsic beauty about true sport—the sweet sound of the ball hitting the fat part of the bat, the geometric arc of the proper golf shot, the thrill of victory and all that goes with it. But in our culture, notions of sport have been corrupted by the huge amounts of money paid to professionals. It is the sweet smell of money, not the sound of the ball hitting the bat, that we crave. Whereas for the artist, the prize is still the excellence of the pursuit.

I have a friend who is a painter. Ted has made his entire adult living with his brush and paints. He graduated from the Chicago Art Institute in the 1920s. In good times and bad, including the Great Depression, Ted stuck to his craft. He has never had a checking account. Once, but only once, he owned an automobile—the gift of a relative. Early in life he saw that the only way to excellence was the unencumbered way. He does not hate money or the things money buys. However, he realized early on that the only way an artist could be true to his craft was to be unencumbered with things that mattered less to him.

We need to have friends like Ted. They remind us of something that we tend to forget because of the obvious economic values attached to work. The paycheck tends to drive everything else from our minds. But no matter how much the world judges our work from "outside," so to speak, and rewards us—or fails to reward us—monetarily, every work has within it the possibility of excellence. Every job can be done poorly, well, or very well indeed.

Match that understanding with the teaching of the Parable of the Pearl Merchant and you reach this insight: *All work has within it "kingdom possibilities."* If human history is marked by the search of God for excellence, then work must have something of this same character. *That person who seeks excellence in whatever he or she does is not far from the kingdom of God.*

That insight is easily corrupted; as soon as it is stated it must be qualified. It does *not* mean that one work is just as good as another, no matter what gifts we have or where we find ourselves. Nor does it necessarily mean that we ought to be content with doing our best, right where we are. Sometimes the search for excellence may lead away from what we are now doing.

My favorite artist in fiction is Thea Kronborg, the hero-
ine of Willa Cather's *The Song of the Lark*. Thea is a
midwestern parson's daughter, who eventually becomes a
world-famous singer. The novel is remarkable for its
description of Thea's single-mindedness. Early in life she
decides that if she is to find success, she will have to put
behind her the busyness of her small town. She sees that
the route to the Metropolitan Opera cannot lead through
playing the piano and singing for the annual strawberry
festival of the Methodist Church. To find what is best for
her, she must forsake what is familiar. And so she leaves
for Chicago.

It is the Theas and Teds of this world who are constant
reminders to us of the excellence that lies hidden in all
work—but also of the need to keep searching. They warn
us of the temptation to sell out for less than the best. They
point to the great treasure that is at the end of life's race,
which is of infinitely greater value than the weekly rewards for the rat race.

4

RETIREMENT
The Parable of the Rich Fool

Contrary to an advertising slogan that was popular some years ago, the future does *not* belong to those who prepare for it today. Nothing we can do in the present can ensure the future. The future is not ours; it is God's. We have today; God has tomorrow. Jesus made that point in an unforgettable way in his Parable of the Rich Fool.

> The land of a rich man brought forth plentifully; and he thought to himself, "What shall I do, for I have nowhere to store my crops?" And he said, "I will do this: I will pull down my barns, and build larger ones; and there I will store all my grain and my goods. And I will say to my soul, Soul, you have ample goods laid up for many years; take your ease, eat, drink, be merry." But God said to him, "Fool! This night your soul is required of you; and the things you have prepared, whose will they be?" So is he who lays up treasure for himself, and is not rich toward God.
>
> (Luke 12:16–21)

Why does Jesus represent God as calling the man a fool? Who is the wise man of our time? Is it not he who has insured his health and his goods and his life against calamity? We consider people to be prudent who store up goods and money against the future. Then why did Jesus call the man in his parable a fool? Because in the biblical understanding of wisdom, the man was indeed foolish. In the way he governed his life, he denied the existence of God.

"The fool says in his heart, 'There is no God'" (Psalm 14:1). In his practical affairs, the rich man denied God's existence. He did not see that his life was not his own but was a loan from the Almighty—and that death hung over his head like a sword on a slender thread. He acted as though he had all the time in the world to plan for his well-being.

And we are equally foolish, the parable implies, if we think that we have lots of time to plan for our enjoyment and are not ready *now* for the Day of Judgment.

The parable does not depend for its effect upon the fact that a man of means was chosen as an example of folly. It was not riches that mattered, but that the man thought, through the piling up of goods, to ensure a happy and fulfilled future. Time, not money, is at issue in the Parable of the Rich Fool. The man thought he had plenty of time when indeed he did not.

All attempts to fashion a secure future by piling up goods, or by planning an estate, or by building an annuity program are based on this false assumption—that we have lots of time at our disposal. Nor is that such a surprising assumption, however false. For it is just against the threat posed by time that we desire to protect ourselves. If we store up enough food, we think, we are insured against a period of famine. If we save enough money, we can ride out a prolonged recession. If we can just put enough by, we can eat and drink and be warm in the most protracted winter—no matter what happens to the crops, to the stock market, or even to our health. Even an extended illness will not drive us to extreme poverty, so long as we have enough money stashed away. To cheat time, that is what we all want to do.

But according to Jesus' parable, all attempts to cheat time are foolish. Time does not stretch before us like a long road, winding endlessly into the future. None of us knows that he or she will be alive tomorrow. If tomorrow you or I should die, what good will estate planning do us? Or food hoarded in our cupboards? Or money invested in tax-free bonds? If we should die tomorrow, what good will it do us to be wealthy as the world counts wealth, but not rich toward God?

In another place in the Gospels, Jesus tells us what it means to be rich toward God. In the Sermon on the Mount, Jesus warns his friends against anxiety about food, clothing, and drink. He says that the Gentiles—unbelievers—seek these things. The faithful are to be distinguished from unbelievers by their seeking something else. And what is that? That which is the major theme of this book—God's kingdom. "But seek first his kingdom and his righteousness, and all these things [food, drink, clothing] shall be yours as well" (Matt. 6:33).

Treasures in Heaven

One of Jesus' most persistent teachings is that we are not to lay up treasures on earth but, rather, treasures in heaven. That woman is truly rich, Jesus taught, who does kindness, loves mercy, and walks humbly with God. That man is truly wealthy whose life abounds in good deeds.

To think to secure one's life through piling up goods or money is a snare and a delusion. What good will the goods do you in the Day of Accounting? No good at all! The reign of God comes as judgment; and how shall those be judged who have been fools in this life, who have denied the existence of God's kingdom by trying to secure their own lives and futures? They will be tried and found wanting.

It is not that the Bible is opposed to eating and drinking and having a good time. That would be a gross misreading of Scripture, as well as a false interpretation of the Parable of the Rich Fool. Much of Jesus' ministry was exercised in eating and drinking and enjoying the company of friends. Let us not allow the Parable of the Rich Fool to be twisted into mean-spirited accusations against those who like a good time or who save their money to buy gourmet food or fine table wines. After all, the scriptural image of the end of history is a great banquet, where the righteous feast in the kingdom with the triumphant Messiah. The most potent symbol the church has of Christ's presence is a meal where bread and wine are enjoyed, both in memory of eating and drinking with him in his earthly life and in anticipation of doing so when he comes again.

We must not pervert the Parable of the Rich Fool into a diatribe against the enjoyment of the good things of life. Rather, the thrust of the parable is that the kingdom comes as suddenly and as finally as death. Those who think to make themselves secure by amassing goods—or who commit themselves to any scheme to cheat time and its ravages—are in for a rude shock. They will discover that the only wealth that counts is being rich toward God. Those who have not known that will be shown to be fools.

Work as Seducer

The temptation to cheat time—to secure the future through one's own efforts— arises out of work itself. Work so easily becomes a seducer whispering in our ear, "If you work harder and earn more money and lay it aside, there will come a time when you will not need to work, when you can eat and drink and be merry—and laugh at those who carry a lunch pail and punch a time clock." Work, which is our partner in the struggle against privation and our helper against want, can take on the role of the seducer, tempting us as it did the rich fool. Its fruitfulness suggests to us that if only we can get more of the fruits of labor, then we can be safe against whatever the future brings. The daily bread that is the reward of work suggests that we might be able to store up enough bread so that we don't need to worry about tomorrow or the day after that or any days in the future.

Certainly we work to earn our daily bread. What is work all about if not to put bread on the table? And not bread only, but meat and cheese and a bottle of wine! Work also puts clothes on our backs and a roof over our heads and provides heat for the winter and cooling from the summer sun. Our labor enables us to eat and drink and enjoy the good world that God has made. We do not labor for labor's sake; we labor to earn our daily bread. We work because we must eat, and because we like to eat and to drink and to be merry with our family and friends.

But along with the provision for daily bread, work brings also a temptation—the temptation to make work into something more than the means of providing bread for today. It brings the temptation to make work to be in some way the provider for the future as well. So that we find ourselves working not only for daily bread but for bread for the day after tomorrow. It is this temptation that Jesus warns us against in his Parable of the Rich Fool.

That temptation seems especially strong for affluent, well-educated, upscale workers in our society. In the 1950s, Sloan Wilson gave us, as a fitting symbol for our time, *The Man in the Gray Flannel Suit*. The central figure in Wilson's novel had to struggle against the efforts of his society, his company, and his job to so absorb his time and energy and emotions that he had nothing left for his family and for himself. The "gray-flannel mind" is all too well known to many of us. We know what it is to be so absorbed in work that we have no time for our families—or for the interior life of mind and spirit.

At the turn of the century in the United States there were two million children under the age of fifteen in the work force. Looking back on those days, we think it inhuman to have robbed those little ones of their childhood—of time for play and of leisure to grow. But today, if a wife or husband works fourteen hours a day, seven days a week, climbing the corporate ladder or pursuing civic causes—leaving no time to be a parent to children or a friend to a spouse—we think it is heroic! Probably in some future time people will look back with appropriate horror on those "superworkers."

There is a limit to what work can do for us. Just as society now wisely sets limits on the labor allowed of children, so God has set limits on the toll demanded of God's children. We are appointed by God to work for our daily bread—but not to secure the future; that is God's work. Why else has God given us the Fourth Commandment, that in six days we shall do all our work, but on the seventh we shall rest? God has put limits on work and on what we do for it and what it does for us. To make work a means of securing the future is ungodly.

The Golden Years

It may come as a shock to some readers to hear the Bible called to witness against efforts to secure one's economic future. It may come as a particular shock to those who are saving for retirement, for those golden years when they can enjoy leisure, travel, and grandchildren without having to earn money to put food on the table.

In our society there has come into being in recent years a new status or life stage called retirement. It is that period between the quitting of regular employment and the time when health and income become uncertain. Retirement has been brought about by a combination of social and economic changes: the Social Security Act, the rise in the level of formal education, the high birthrate that followed World War II, better health services. For some, retirement may last as long as twenty years. There is plenty of money for travel, for leisure pursuits, for the cultivation of friendships and the deepening of family ties In many respects it is indeed a golden age. And why not plan for it? One personnel specialist said of his clients: "Most people spend more time planning for a two-week vacation than they do for their retirement!"

However, the Parable of the Rich Fool warns us against counting on a golden age. If golden years are allotted to us, they are to be considered a bonus—not a right. No one can count on having fifteen or twenty such years granted to him or her. We must not neglect travel, friendship, and family ties *now* in the fond hope that "later, when we retire, we'll have time and money for those things."

The future is not ours; it is God's. If a golden age is granted any of us during those so-called retirement years, it comes as a gift. It is not a reward for hard work.

A Negative Example

But that is all so negative! Has the Parable of the Rich Fool nothing positive to give us as a pattern for the workplace? No. There is no way to derive directly from the parable a model for the Christian worker. The Rich Fool is one of those parables of Jesus that are intended as examples. In this case, the example is a negative one. It would be a misreading of Scripture and a misuse of Jesus' parables to interpret it any other way. The Rich Fool must remain for us a warning, a negative model, a caution against doing what he did.

The parable leaves us with a warning, but also with a choice. One must finally choose: Which is the true wisdom and which the folly? Is it wisdom to be content to work for the bread that one needs today for oneself and one's family? To be content if one has enough now to eat and drink and wear? Or is it true wisdom to work as hard as possible—with all one's energy and strength—to store up against an uncertain future, to ensure against drought, depression, ill health, or other possible disasters?

If Jesus' parable is to be believed, we cannot have it both ways. If we hold that true wisdom is to be rich toward God, then work will have a limited place in our lives. *We shall work hard enough to provide the necessities; we shall leave the future in God's hands.* We will not make work a means of securing our lives against all possible calamities.

But if we think that true wisdom is to know that indeed the future *is* uncertain, that one can never have too much saved up against a rainy day—or a sick day—then we will make a primary goal of work the amassing of as much goods and insurance and invested wealth as possible. There will never be enough savings, profits, investments, goods, achievements, insurance policies, or tax-free municipal bonds in the safe-deposit box. Like the man who was unable to follow Jesus because he had too much money, we shall turn away from the demands and the promises of God's kingdom.

Do you remember that man? He was so eager to hear the formula for the good life that he ran after Jesus. When he had caught up, he stopped the Teacher in his tracks by kneeling in front of him. Then he asked, panting, "Good Teacher, what must I do to inherit eternal life?" Jesus told him what to do, which the man already knew: Keep God's commandments. And the man vowed that from his youth he had done just that. Jesus said to him, "You lack one thing: go, sell what you have, and give to the poor, and you will have treasure in heaven; and come, follow me." And the man turned away, sorrowful, for he was very wealthy (cf. Mark 10:17–22). He chose not to follow Jesus. He was a first-century man in a gray-flannel suit. His heart was captive to the false promises of money.

owner of the vineyard said to his steward, "Call the
laborers and pay them their wages, beginning with
the last, up to the first." And when those hired about
the eleventh hour came, each of them received a
denarius. Now when the first came, they thought
they would receive more; but each of them also received a denarius. And on receiving it they grum-
bled at the householder, saying, "These last worked
only one hour, and you have made them equal to us
who have borne the burden of the day and the
scorching heat." But he replied to one of them,
"Friend, I am doing you no wrong; did you not agree
with me for a denarius? Take what belongs to you,
and go; I choose to give to this last as I give to you.
Am I not allowed to do what I choose with what
belongs to me? Or do you begrudge my generosity?"
(Matthew 20:1–15)

The Parable of the Workers in the Vineyard provides us
with a tantalizing peek at an economy in which each
worker is adequately compensated, yet in which the basic
needs of each are also met. We are wise enough not to
read Jesus' parables as blueprints for a new economic
order. Yet in this one parable there is a hint—possibly
even a preview—of economic justice that transcends our
present understanding.

Economic Justice

Put those two words "economic" and "justice" side by
side, and you start a fight. The phrase "economic justice"
divides our world into warring camps. On the one side are
those who understand such justice in terms of rewards or

compensation. To them, a just order is one in which each is fairly paid or compensated according to his or her productive work. Their slogan is, "Those who will eat, let them work."

But there are also those who give primacy to the equal distribution of goods and services. To them there is no justice in a system where some go to bed hungry while others scrape excess food into garbage disposals. Their slogan is, "From each according to ability; to each according to need."

The geographic gulf that divides these two camps is no wider than the 235 air miles separating Havana from Miami. Socialist Cuba boasts of its more equal distribution of food, housing, education, jobs, and health services, while in Miami there are those who fled the Cuban revolution, arriving in the United States with nothing, and who in a few years were able to establish businesses, get superior educations, and rise to offices of great responsibility. The spiritual and intellectual gulf that separates these two camps is enormous. The terms "free enterprise" and "socialism" identify the two camps but do not truly define them. The phrases "compensatory justice" and "distributive justice" may also be oversimplifications, but they are less loaded terms.

In his Parable of the Workers in the Vineyard, Jesus seems to imply an order of justice that goes beyond contemporary notions, whether these be characterized as free enterprise vs. socialism or compensatory vs. distributive justice. And yet Jesus' ideal of justice would exclude neither. All persons are given a fair compensation for work done; all get what they need for subsistence. If this new kind of justice had a motto, it might be: "To each as he or she has contributed; to each also according to individual need."

This is not the same as the socialist idea, in which each is rewarded according to need, no matter how small or great the contribution to the common good. In his book *The Russians*, Hedrick Smith reports a conversation with a Soviet citizen on the subject of retirement. The man showed no fear of growing old, Smith said, for he knew that the state guaranteed him an income and medical care, whether or not he continued to be productive.

Jesus' Parable of the Workers in the Vineyard cannot be made into an argument for simple distributive justice. For in his story each worker went into the vineyard and did the labor assigned, with no expectation that all would be equally rewarded. In fact, those who went at six in the morning and worked a full twelve hours were morally outraged that those who went at five in the afternoon also got a full day's pay! The parable makes it quite clear that the workers were not rewarded according to some new notion of a fair day's wage. Rather, it was the generosity of the owner that accounted for each one's getting the same amount of money.

But neither can the parable be decoded to favor Western notions of economic justice, according to which those who take full advantage of their opportunities are allowed a larger share of goods and services. For our Western ideal differs from that of the socialist world; we hope to offer to everyone equal opportunity, but then we also hope to reward those who take the fullest advantage of that opportunity. Our folk heroes are not the industrial workers, toiling all day in the heat and dirt and sweat of a steel mill, knowing they are counted as worthy as the commissar who sits at a desk. No, our folk heroes are the men and women who start out in life with nothing and work their way up the corporate ladder to the top rung.

But in the Parable of the Workers in the Vineyard, all who work—no matter how much or how little—share equally in the rewards. Those who went at six in the morning and those who went at five in the afternoon receive a full day's pay. In the economy of Jesus' day, a day's wage was equivalent to what a family needed for subsistence. So that in his parable, all workers did what they were asked to do, and all received enough to provide for their families. A very strange sort of compensatory system indeed! Not at all like the notion of justice that governs our economic dealings one with another.

Jesus' story of the workers in the vineyard has a counterpart in the Old Testament. In 1 Samuel 30, there is the story of David's victory over the Amalekites. They had attacked his camp in his absence and had carried off persons and property. In the course of pursuing the enemy, a third of David's army tired and was left behind to tend the baggage. When the rest returned with the recaptured property—and considerable booty to boot—some of the lions who had fought the final battle wanted to give to the baggage tenders a mouse's share of the loot. David would have none of that. He made sure that all shared and shared alike in the plunder. To those who would deny to the baggage tenders their equal share, he said, "You shall not do so, my brothers, with what the LORD has given to us; he has preserved us and given into our hand the band that came against us" (1 Sam. 30:23).

David based his distribution of goods on the prior, gracious gift of God. Likewise, in Jesus' parable it is the generosity of the owner of the vineyard that determines the wages each will receive. Jesus implies a future in which both compensatory *and* distributive schemes are transcended by a new economic order, grounded not on notions of what is fair only or needful only but on the graciousness of God.

The early church seems to have sensed something of this kind of new order. For it is written of the first Christians:

> And all who believed were together and had all things in common; and they sold their possessions and goods and distributed them to all, as any had need. And day by day, attending the temple together and breaking bread in their homes, they partook of food with glad and generous hearts, praising God and having favor with all the people.
>
> (Acts 2:44–47)

In that fleeting, brief glimpse of a new kind of social order, note the emphasis on generosity, thankfulness, and the prior gifts of God. For a moment the curtain that hides us from the future is pulled aside; we are permitted to see how humanity, under God, might live.

What of Us?

But that better future has not yet arrived; that new day has not yet dawned. We live in a world that neither rewards labor fairly nor distributes goods and services adequately. The economic systems of both West and East are seriously flawed. Those who go early into the vineyard tend to get more than their fair share; those who are late to be called—because of class or color or bad luck—often get less than they need. So where does the Parable of the

Workers in the Vineyard fit into our world? Or, rather,
where do we fit into the Parable of the Workers?

Oh, we can find ourselves in the narrative with no
trouble at all! We are like the laborers who put in a full
twelve hours' work and then groused when the others
who worked fewer hours were paid the same. One of the
characteristics of the workplace—as we know it—is that
neither is there equal pay for the same work nor a fair
distribution of goods in relation to unequal work. Factors
such as caste, color, genes, sex, luck, and favoritism always conspire to keep the scales of justice out of balance.

There is no truly equal reward system operating in this
world; none of us gets a truly fair shake. Two farmers
plant the same crop; each rises early, works long hours,
falls into bed at night exhausted. One has a bumper harvest; locusts come and eat the other's wheat. Parents lavish love and care and braces and dancing lessons on two
daughters: one rewards them by becoming a brain sur-
geon; the other breaks their hearts by turning her brain to
mush with drugs. The world does not pay equal wages. In
many an office there is one secretary who turns every
coffee break into a mini vacation, while another works
beyond all expectations. Both receive the same pay.

One of the reasons we have learned not to give our
whole hearts to our work is that it is never rewarded
fairly. Who wants to be played for a sucker? The world of
work seems to know nothing of the finer points of either
compensatory or distributive justice. Think about your
own workplace. Don't you know at least one person who
gets away with murder? And whose salary is equal to—or
more than—yours? Of course you do. And the same is
true of every factory, faculty, bureau, business, system, or
store. Some workers bear the heat and burden of the day;

others do a bare minimum. If we dwell too long on comparisons, we quickly fall into envy, anger, and cynicism.

To the temptation to be cynical about rewards, the Parable of the Workers in the Vineyard speaks a direct word: *You do not labor in vain if you put in a full day's work; it is not foolish to live up to your end of the bargain with your employer.* The future does not belong to the clock-watchers, the time-servers, the lazy, the goof-offs, the deadbeats, the chiselers. It belongs to one, like the employer in the parable, who is just as well as generous. *You work with the future, not against it, if you do what is asked of you*—whether you go into the fields at six in the morning or at five in the afternoon.

But is the parable simply an exhortation to us all to work hard? Lord forbid that we read it so! For then we should be guilty of perverting a message about the grace of God into a morality tale. The parable is not about hard work; it is about a remarkable reward system. It speaks not of what we ought to do but of a new order of justice for which we may hope.

To Serve a Vision

What can we do, here and now, to serve that hope? There are some current experiments that are reaching for the order of justice hinted at in Jesus' parable. In small groups in communes, in factories, and on farms there are workers who are trying to prove that labor may be rewarded according to both merit and need. Such experiments, however, tend to repeat the patterns of earlier societies, such as the hunting society of the Eskimo. When there was a seal hunt, everyone shared in the distribution of meat. The shares were not precisely equal;

the man who harpooned the seal got the choicest portion. One cannot, after all, slice up a seal like a salami! But everyone got what each needed to survive. It was no disgrace not to have taken part in the hunt, to have stayed behind to tend the baggage. But it is sentimentalism to suppose that we can turn back the calendar to the days of hunting societies. Any pattern of rewards must work in large as well as in small systems.

Instead of turning back the calendar, can we flip it ahead? Some science fiction writers have tried to paint a more just social order. In her novel *The Dispossessed*, Ursula Le Guin describes life on the planet Anarres. Anarres has been colonized by followers of the philosopher/prophet Odo. Odians are anarchists; in their society there is no government, no hierarchy, not even private property. Living is wholly voluntary, wholly communal. Each chooses what work he or she will do—if any. All share common meals and free housing. The central figure of the novel is a brilliant physicist, who builds a theory that will lead to instant communication, across lightyears. Such a new system might help Anarres in its struggle against a harsh environment. But the physicist is held back by jealous persons who accuse him of being an "egoizer." His child is bullied at school; his own mother opposes him. Even in that utopian society no way is found to allow full freedom to persons with extraordinary gifts. Equality becomes the enemy of truth.

However, the Parable of the Workers in the Vineyard does suggest a pattern that might work in any economic system, large or small. That pattern is provided by the vineyard owner, who manages to deal honorably with each worker, yet who meets the needs of each. In him we see justice and charity walking hand in hand. His activity may be exemplary for our own. It may be possible for each of us to be both just and generous in our work relationships.

Suppose we were to take the vineyard owner as our model. Then we might, for example, cease to be purse-strung by absolute standards. Many parents do not give their children allowances. "I'm old-fashioned," a father says. "I believe that a person ought to work for every cent." But the example of the vineyard owner makes that attitude seem indeed not only old-fashioned, but after the fashion of a world that is passing away.

To that fading world also belongs the resistance of present employers to schemes that would make the workplace more humane—day-care centers for employees' children, four-day workweeks for working parents. A four-day week might not only allow working couples to spend more time with their children, it might also cut down on energy consumption in offices and factories. But many employers regard the four-day workweek as a gimmick, an attempt of the work force to get something for nothing. Many of these same employers regard day-care centers as the parents' problem—certainly no concern of business or industry.

If we had Jesus' vineyard owner as our example, we might not be so afraid of being considered "soft" with fellow workers. We might be more generous in allowing them time off for personal affairs, less quick to judge them harshly. In short, we might get rid of some of those tired maxims that conceal a mean-spirited approach to rewards, "There is no such thing as a free lunch" and "The early bird gets the worm." Instead, we would be ruled by a more gracious spirit.

For behind the figure of the employer in the parable—like the reality behind a shadow—is the figure of God whom we know in Jesus Christ. God has not distributed to us goods or health or friends or opportunities only according to merit. In dealing with us, God has transcended all human notions of fair play or square deals. If God has been so generous with us, can we be less than generous in dealing with others in the workplace?

During a year spent as an army clerk, I served two masters. Both were warrant officers, both regular army, both committed to the system; neither wanted to subvert it. Yet one I loved, the other I hated. The first, whose name—ironically—was Self, found ways to stretch the army system to make it relatively humane for us draftees. The other—whose name I have deliberately repressed—found ways to use the system to make our lives miserable. Mr. Self proved to me that it is possible, even within a large and rigid system, to make that system more humane, more just, more rewarding. That would seem to be the message for us of the Parable of the Workers in the Vineyard. Until the new order arrives, we can stretch the old order to make it more rewarding and more just for all who work in it.

6

WASTE
The Parable
of the Prodigal Son

"Waste not, want not." That is bumper-sticker wisdom.
It is also sound advice. Who could disagree? It is sage
advice for the butcher, the baker, the candlestick maker—and also for the housewife, the attorney, the student,
the merchant, and the retiree. A wasteful worker is an
unfaithful worker. Work is the enemy of waste, waste is
the father of want.

Yet God is wasteful—prodigally wasteful. That is the
teaching of Jesus' Parable of the Loving Father, more
popularly know as the Parable of the Prodigal Son.

> There was a man who had two sons; and the younger
> of them said to his father, "Father, give me the share
> of property that falls to me." And he divided his
> living between them. Not many days later, the
> younger son gathered all he had and took his jour-
> ney into a far country, and there he squandered his
> property in loose living. And when he had spent
> everything, a great famine arose in that country, and
> he began to be in want. So he went and joined him-
> self to one of the citizens of that country, who sent
> him into his fields to feed swine. And he would glad-
> ly have fed on the pods that the swine ate; and

no one gave him anything. But when he came to himself he said, "How many of my father's hired servants have bread enough and to spare, but I perish here with hunger! I will arise and go to my father, and I will say to him, 'Father, I have sinned against heaven and before you; I am no longer worthy to be called your son; treat me as one of your hired servants.'" And he arose and came to his father. But while he was yet at a distance, his father saw him and had compassion, and ran and embraced him and kissed him. And the son said to him, "Father, I have sinned against heaven and before you; I am no longer worthy to be called your son." But the father said to his servants, "Bring quickly the best robe, and put it on him; and put a ring on his hand, and shoes on his feet; and bring the fatted calf and kill it, and let us eat and make merry; for this my son was dead, and is alive again; he was lost, and is found." And they began to make merry.

Now his elder son was in the field; and as he came and drew near to the house, he heard music and dancing. And he called one of the servants and asked what this meant. And he said to him, "Your brother has come, and your father has killed the fatted calf, because he has received him safe and sound." But he was angry and refused to go in. His father came out and entreated him, but he answered his father, "Lo, these many years I have served you, and I never disobeyed your command; yet you never gave me a kid, that I might make merry with my friends. But when this son of yours came, who has devoured your living with harlots, you killed for him the fatted calf!" And he said to him, "Son, you are always with

me, and all that is mine is yours. It was fitting to
make merry and be glad, for this your brother was
dead, and is alive; he was lost, and is found."

(Luke 15:11–32)

If Jesus had ended his story with the return of the
younger son, we would follow tradition and call it the
Parable of the Prodigal Son. But the narrative is about a
father who had two boys. And when we have read the
entire biblical passage, we understand that the main character in the parable is the parent and not the younger
brother.

A useful rule to follow in the interpretation of the parables of Jesus is that of "end stress." The point that Jesus
wanted to make is most likely to be found at or near the
end of the story. In Luke 15:11–32, the emphasis at the
end of the narrative is clearly on the father and his forgiv-
ing love. So the main point of the parable, we believe, is
not about the wastefulness of the son but rather about the
extravagant love of his father.

But is the parable only about love? Isn't it also about
waste? Isn't the father in the story dreadfully wasteful?
What are we to say about a parent who turns over to a
seventeen-year-old son his total inheritance and allows
him to squander it as he pleases? (In Jesus' society the
usual marriage age for men was in the range of eighteen
to twenty. The fact that the younger son seems as yet to
be unmarried would indicate that Jesus had in mind a
person of tender years.) In our society, a father would be
marked down as wasteful who allowed what was permitted the son in the parable.

In Jesus' society, that would have been even more the
case. For in an agricultural society, land—property—was

everything. The neighbors of a father would have regarded it a piece of colossal folly to turn loose in the world an underage son with his entire patrimony at stake. That would have seemed extravagance on a grand scale.

Tradition has already branded the younger son a prodigal—a wastrel. We have heard the story so often that our hearts are calloused to its tragic elements. When the younger boy threw away his money, it was not only money that he lost, it was his stake. It represented his one and only chance in life to be someone and to do something. Managing his inheritance was to be his life's work, his occupation. Once he let his capital slip through his fingers, it was gone forever. The modern parallel is that son or daughter of a good family who, instead of getting an education, chooses to damage his or her mind with drugs and forever after is good for little but the most menial of jobs.

And what of the older brother in the parable? What do we know of him? Mostly that he despised waste. He knew all about "waste not, want not." For him it was not mere bumper-sticker wisdom, it was his life's creed. He had never asked his father for so much as a kid that he might have a party with his friends. Nor could he see his father's forgiveness of his brother as anything but grand waste! (He may have been right. Who is to say that such a younger brother would ever amount to anything at all, that he would not make waste of a second chance, or a third, or a fourth? From what we know of persons of his kind—life's losers—it is unlikely that he would ever be anything but a prodigal.)

An Open Question

The question remains open: Is the parable primarily about love or is it also about waste? Should we call it the Parable of the Loving Father, or should we call it the Parable of the Wasteful Father? It is well to leave that question open. Jesus himself seems to have wanted the parable to leave his hearers with that question to ponder and to resolve for themselves. Most likely he told the story in the first place to those who prided themselves on being hard workers and on having earned the love of their Heavenly Father—and who openly despised Jesus for wasting his time with ne'er-do-wells and no-accounts.

We know that Jesus spent much of his time with those whom the good folk regarded as human waste: tax collectors, prostitutes, beggars, the incurably ill. And did not Jesus say that the realm of God was open to them, that indeed many of them would enter it before the "superworkers," the scribes and Pharisees who labored so hard to do all that God commanded?

It is quite likely that Jesus wanted the hearers of the parable to go away wondering, Is it wasteful of God to be merciful to outcasts and derelicts, to those who have wasted their lives? Is it prodigal of God to open the realm of heaven to persons like the returning wastrel in the story?

These are not easy questions to answer—not for us, anyway. We have a natural sympathy for the older brother, no matter how much we want to think of God as a loving parent. We hate waste—the waste of opportunity, the waste of money, the waste of an inheritance. Especially we hate the waste of youth! We agree with George Bernard Shaw that youth is too good to be wasted on the

young. What is more precious? And we may even feel
contempt for the father who lavished love on a son who
obviously despised him. For if the younger son did not
hate his father, why go to such lengths—and dis-
tances—to break his father's heart? Why else would a
Jewish boy find himself feeding unclean animals and
dreaming of being one of his father's hired hands, unless
at some point he had not deliberately turned his back on
his father and all that his father loved—his cultural heritage, his Jewishness? Is not love for such an ungrateful
and hateful son wasted?

We have contemporary counterparts to the prodigal
son—those unfortunates one sees in bus and train sta-
tions, begging on the streets, lying in the gutters, carrying
all their worldly possessions in shopping bags, locked
away in drunk tanks, tossed into prisons. They have no
real future; we know that. We could more easily imagine
the prodigal in Jesus' parable leaving off being a swine-
herd and becoming his father's hired hand than we could
envision one of those poor people holding down a responsible job. What are they good for? we wonder. They are
"wastepersons." Why doesn't someone come with a giant
broom and sweep them up and dispose of them? Why
should we, who work hard for our money, support them
with our taxes or even our charity? Once they may have
had a chance in life—everybody does—but they threw
their chances away. Why waste pity on them?

If we admit to such feelings and thoughts, we also will
question whether the kingdom of God is open to losers.
The possibility casts a cloud over our own efforts to work
hard and to be responsible and respectable citizens. If we
answer, Yes, God loves the wastepersons, then why do we
work so hard not to be like those people in the bus sta-

tions, the gutters, the drunk tanks? How can God care for them as much as for us? Isn't God a worker? Didn't God work for six days to create the world, before resting on the seventh? And did not God command us to work six days before allowing us a day of leisure?

Nevertheless, God *does* seem to lean a bit to the side of those whom the world despises and counts as waste. It was so with Israel. When God loved Israel and took the people to be God's Chosen, Israel was nothing. As the faithful Israelite learned to recite:

> A wandering Aramean was my father; and he went down into Egypt and sojourned there, few in number; and there he became a nation, great, mighty, and populous. And the Egyptians treated us harshly, and afflicted us, and laid upon us hard bondage. Then we cried to the LORD the God of our fathers, and the LORD heard our voice, and saw our affliction, our toil, and our oppression; and the LORD brought us out of Egypt with a mighty hand and an outstretched arm, with great terror, with signs and wonders.
>
> (Deuteronomy 26:5–8)

Most of Jesus' ministry consisted of being with and around persons whom society despised or ignored: tax collectors, lepers, prostitutes—the kind of folk that the hardworking could scarcely abide. He summoned Peter, Andrew, James, and John to leave honest work as fishermen to be with him in his ministry. Surely their fathers must have thought their sons were wasting their lives to go with an itinerant rabbi! Jesus had continually to defend himself against the charge that he consorted with drunkards and good-for-nothings. Very likely the Parable of the Loving Father was a rebuttal to such charges.

The apostle Paul could write to a congregation of Christians who were the scum—not the cream—of the Roman Empire:

> For consider your call, brethren; not many of you were wise according to worldly standards, not many were powerful, not many were of noble birth; but God chose what is foolish in the world to shame the wise, God chose what is weak in the world to shame the strong, God chose what is low and despised in the world, even things that are not, to bring to nothing things that are.
>
> (1 Corinthians 1:26–28)

The question that Jesus raised in our parable—Does God lean to the side of wastepersons?—is not only an open question. It is also a pressing one. For if God is like the father in the parable, then does not God also favor the derelict, the shopping-bag lady, the gutter drunk? And, if so, how can God countenance such waste?

Waste and Work

No one who works for a living can be indifferent to that question. For waste is the enemy of work. Work, by definition, is a war on waste. Work means taking something that would otherwise go to waste—time, land, wood, ore, petroleum—and making it yield that which is of use or profit to humankind. Don't we measure work in terms of time—hours that would otherwise be wasted? It is hard to think of labor without thinking of waste.

In the story that Scripture unfolds, humankind is consigned to a life of toil, defined in terms of waste and want. After the man and woman had eaten the forbidden fruit and were about to be expelled from the garden, God said to them:

> Cursed is the ground because of you;
>   in toil you shall eat of it all the days of your life;
> thorns and thistles it shall bring forth to you;
>   and you shall eat the plants of the field.
>   (Genesis 3:17–18)

After the Fall, land that once brought forth fruit without human effort now was wasteland—"thorns and thistles." Only great human effort would make it yield the plants that humans need for survival.

When I was a child, growing up in the Great Depression, it was not uncommon for a tramp or a hobo to come to the back door of our house, asking for something to eat. Grandma would always make a sandwich for such a person, who would eat it while sitting on the back steps. We children would watch through the kitchen window. To us, tramps were glamorous. They didn't have to wash before meals or do anything else they didn't want to. They traveled around and saw the world. But none of the adults in town found tramps attractive; quite the opposite. Tramps were the enemy: They did not work; they lived from the labor of others. Children were to be kept away from them. Tramps were held up to us as warnings of what might happen if we did not apply ourselves at school. They were pitied as well as feared, for they seemed not to know that God had called humankind to toil for food and drink.

Therefore, if we accept as the teaching of the Parable of the Loving Father that God leans on the side of wastrels and tramps, that has got to be received as a hard teaching indeed!

The Workplace

Let us assume that in some sense whether or not God leans a bit on the side of prodigals is still an open question. What does that mean for the worker and the workplace? If we translate our question into one that has immediate relevance for us, it reads like this: Is there any room in the workplace for mercy? Does the loving father in Jesus' parable provide a pattern for the Christian worker? Or must the workplace by its very nature always be unforgiving of waste, inefficiency, and the squandering of time, goods, and talents? Does the God who is a loving father belong only in the confessional, the sanctuary, the counseling session? Or does such a God belong also in the place of work?

The questions are crucial, not only for the Christian worker but for theology. If the mercy of God is not relevant to the workplace, then the realm of religion has shrunk considerably. If there is no room for mercy in the workplace, there cannot be room there for the God of the Bible, who is merciful. So how will we answer those questions?

Certainly Jesus wanted the original hearers of his parable to understand that God leans a bit on the side of the younger brothers of society, that there is a place in God's kingdom for the good-for-nothing as well as for the faithful and obedient.

If that is so, the loving father provides us with a useful pattern for the workplace. For one thing, those of us who work may have mercy upon ourselves! We can forgive the "younger brother" who is in each of us, for we would not hate and fear the wastepersons in society were there not some trace of that sort of person lurking within us.

It is doubtful that Jesus intended the two sons in his story to represent two tendencies in human nature. But we do know that within each of us live both the younger and the elder brother. Each of us is a potential prodigal, who yearns to be free from the restrictions of job and home and prudence and saving, who longs for the open road, for the far country, for the big gamble, for throwing everything to the winds to see where it will blow.

We need to be kind to that prodigal within, lest we punish ourselves for not always living up to our own high standards of performance and conformity. How many gray-flannel personalities are driven to the outer limits of psychic and physical exhaustion, trying to prove to themselves that they are *not* prodigal daughters or sons, trying to put to death the wastrel within?

We also need to have mercy on our fellow workers. There is also within us an elder brother—or sister—who judges harshly those who do not live up to our own high standards of performance and conformity. Who of us does not know the stab of hate turned outward toward the other? Who does not resent the other's coffee break, her vacation, his arriving at work late, her reading novels on the job, his going home before the work is done?

Such censoriousness is poison to human relations in the workplace. It drives wedges between workers, just as in the parable it drove a wedge between the two brothers.

(Note that when the younger boy came home, the other referred to him as "this son of yours," not as "my brother.") Such judgmental attitudes deny a fundamental biblical teaching, that it is not through good works that we are saved, but through the unmerited grace of God. God loves both the younger brother and the elder brother in each of us—and in the other. God is like the father in the parable, who yearns over both sons and has room for both in the realm of heaven.

The workplace, which knows all too well the wasteful tendencies of the younger son and the harshness of the elder, needs also the extravagant love of the father. Such mercy can season the workplace and make it more humane. It can bring peace to the inner warfare of the individual worker. It can bring peace between the overachievers and those who fall far short of perfection. We do not have to choose between the two sons. We may choose to be like the father.

7

FULFILLMENT
The Parable
of the Mustard Seed

Reading the Parable of the Mustard Seed is like slipping into a pair of old shoes. At once we feel at home. Jesus' story of the tiny seed that grew into a great shrub transports us into a world we have known since childhood. It is the world where great oaks from little acorns grow, where a journey of a thousand miles begins with a single step, and where a wee pebble tossed into a pond sends ripples to the farthest shore.

How easily we are tricked into comfort! Surely Jesus' intention in telling the Parable of the Mustard Seed was to snatch his hearers out of the everyday world of acorns and oaks and to confront them with the otherworldly kingdom of God.

"'The kingdom of heaven," Jesus taught, "is like a grain of mustard seed which a man took and sowed in his field; it is the smallest of all seeds, but when it has grown it is the greatest of shrubs and becomes a tree, so that the birds of the air come and make nests in its branches" (Matt. 13:31–32).

Jesus' fancy was seized by the absurd disproportion between the mustard plant as sown and that same plant as grown. Such a huge shrub from such a small seed! The difference seemed not so much a natural progression as a quantum jump. Therefore he saw the growth of the mustard seed as an apt simile for the reign of God, for the reign of God promises a fulfillment out of all proportion to its observable beginnings.

What we have witnessed of the reign of God in the ministry of Jesus—or what we now think to see of that reign in the ministry of Christ's church—is not a forecast of what we shall yet receive. What is waiting for us, up ahead in God's better future, is not the good made better and the better made best. The realm of God is a state of affairs far exceeding all reasonable expectations. As the mature plant must shock the imaginations of those who know only its insignificant beginnings, so the kingdom is far more grand than anything we can now suppose.

The Strange World of Scripture

The Parable of the Mustard Seed thrusts us into the strange world of the Bible. It is the world in which God once came to childless Abraham and told him to turn his eyes to the sky: "Look toward heaven, and number the stars. . . . So shall your descendants be" (Gen. 15:5). And when Abraham was a hundred years old—presumably seedless—and his wife nearly as old, a son was born to them. And from that seedling grew the great people whom we know as Israel.

As historians calculate such matters, Abraham was of no more significance than one grain of sand on a vast seashore. He lived in the nearly empty space between two great cultures: the Sumerian to the east and the Egyptian to the south. What was one nomad measured against these monumental civilizations? What is a gnat between two elephants? And yet it was to Abraham, and not to the

Egyptians or Sumerians, that God said, "I will indeed bless you, and I will multiply your descendants as . . . the sand which is on the seashore" (Gen. 22:17).

One of those descendants of Abraham and Sarah was Jesus of Nazareth. When Jesus saw that the hour of his death was near, he said to his friends, "Unless a grain of wheat falls into the earth and dies, it remains alone; but if it dies, it bears much fruit" (John 12:24). Surely not even Jesus could foresee the magnitude of the changes to be wrought in the world because of his being planted in the tomb. The effect of the life and death of Jesus upon Western civilization is beyond calculation. The billions who have borne his name are but part of that story. The influence of Christian ideas and ideals is immeasurable. One could reverse the equation and say that without the life and death of Jesus, modern civilization itself is unthinkable.

The apostle Paul once meditated on the cosmic meaning of the sufferings of Christ. He wrote, "The creation itself will be set free from its bondage to decay and obtain the glorious liberty of the children of God" (Rom. 8:21). What Paul foresaw as the consequence of Jesus' reconciling death was nothing less than the liberation of the entire created order from decay and death. That is a consequence of such magnitude—so out of proportion to the event of the crucifixion—as to be well beyond representing to the imagination.

Let us suppose that Ernest Becker is right in the argument that he advances in *The Denial of Death*—that human life can best be characterized as an attempt to deny the reality of death. What might it then be like for human beings —not to mention the rest of creation—to be freed from the threat of death? Who can say? Who can picture it?

Who of us, then, can imagine the entire universe loosed from the law of decay and death? The reign of God in all its fullness will be a reordering of creation, a different arrangement of oaks and acorns, of journeys and steps. The seer of the book of Revelation could speak of "a new heaven and a new earth" (Rev. 21:1). But that is all we can now know. There is no way that the mind can calculate and represent the final triumph of God—any more than we could, given only a tiny seed to contemplate, have imagined it growing into a great shrub!

Each a Sower

We do not yet, however, live in that new world. We live and do our work in a world where indeed great oaks from little acorns grow, and, yes, where a journey of a thousand miles begins with a single step. And besides, what is so unusual about a large plant growing from a tiny seed? The metaphor is familiar to all of us. Our very civilization is based upon the discovery that plants grow from seeds. That was the insight that freed our forebears from being hunters and gatherers and allowed them to become farmers. It was settled agriculture—most likely begun in the Middle East before the time of Abraham—that made civilization possible.

The metaphor of the plant growing from the tiny seed is basic to everyday thinking. Parenting is the daily sowing of commands and ideas and words, in the confidence that they will someday flower into fixed habits and characters. The salesperson plants little smiles and handshakes in the hope of one day closing a big deal. The single vote that the politician elicits with a handshake multiplies to become a majority vote in that election district. Teachers drill pupils in their ABC's in the confidence that one day they will be able to read encyclopedias.

Even the work of the Christian ministry, which we may suppose to be exemplary for the labor of all Christians, is a matter of sowing tiny seeds. We Christians cannot, by taking thought—or by raising money or electing official boards—make a single disciple, build a single congregation, or advance the cause of human rights one iota. We can no more establish the kingdom of God by our own efforts than we can make a tree! We can tell the good news, appeal for righteousness in the public sector, and speak out against injustice and cruelty. But there is no guarantee that these efforts will produce a more just society.

All of us sow seeds—nothing more. If we wanted to mint a coin to symbolize that money represents the fruits of labor, what might we stamp on that coin? We could do no better than to depict a sower on one side and a flourishing crop on the other. Work is mostly the sowing of tiny seeds and the hope for large results.

Anyone who supposes that he or she is more than a sower of seeds should know about copy editors. In the publishing business—books, magazines, newspapers—there are those who take the authors' manuscripts and correct their mistakes. When a copy editor gets through with a typical typewritten page, that sheet of paper looks as though a chicken had walked across it after first wading in ink. A writer may be able to fool the public—but not the copy editor. Suppose that you have written, "Waiting for his wife to come out of the store, the baseball game on the car radio kept him amused."

Now the reading public knows exactly what is meant by that sentence. But a copy editor knows that it contains a dangling participle and will fix it—and may even write in the margin a snide comment for the author, such as, "How often have you seen baseball games waiting in shopping centers?"

We all have someone looking over our shoulders, waiting to correct small mistakes. Authors have copy editors. Students have teachers to grade their papers. Bankers have auditors. Lathe operators have inspectors. Each person who fills out a Form 1040 has the Internal Revenue Service. No matter what we do, we cannot escape the tyranny of minute details. There are no big jobs; there are only seemingly large tasks made up of many small operations. None of us is permitted to go through life dealing only with important matters. We all are sowers of seeds. The workplace is, by analogy, a field where each day tiny seeds are planted, in the hope that they will grow and flourish and flower into large results.

A Door Between

If that is so, the workplace cannot be far from the kingdom of God. The world of work and the otherworldly reign of God must be close to each other. There must be a way to move from one to the other; there must be a door between. Does the Parable of the Mustard Seed furnish us with a message about our daily work? Does it provide us with a mirror where we may see our better selves?

A mirror, no; a message, yes. We do not need a mirror to show us what we already know too well about the workplace. We know that we are employed as sowers of seeds; we do not need to be exhorted to keep on doing what we cannot change. But the parable of the tiny seed grown into a great shrub does have a message for us: *Do not despise yourself or fall into despair when you do only small things. Concealed in, with, and under what seem to you to be insignificant acts is the better future that God intends for us.*

The Christian worker, most especially, is apt to be driven to despair—or to its pernicious twin, apathy—by the great gap that yawns between the vision of perfection and the performance. We want to do great things for God; we do not seem to do even average-sized things for God. When we cannot see a realistic link between the goals of the kingdom and our own small ineffective efforts, we easily lapse into self-accusation and then indifference.

I once served as chairperson of a task force that was committed to building low-income housing in a middle-class community. All the means to our end were in place: low-interest federal loans, free consultation services, the backing of community churches. Although for several months we met weekly to plan and organize, we never built a single house. We on that task force could never quite convince ourselves that building a few houses was a worthy part of Lyndon Johnson's War on Poverty.

By contrast, one of the most admirable attacks on human need is the home-building program of Koinonia Farms, Americus, Georgia. The members of that project are content to build homes for the poor of their community, one at a time. When completed, a new house is sold on a long-term contract to persons of low income, and the project members start work on another house. It seems a simplistic way to attack the problem of the world's homeless. But it is wholly consistent with the teaching of Scripture that in this world we can be but sowers of seed.

Consider also the challenge to the Christian community from the reality of world hunger. Every night millions upon millions of the world's children go to bed with empty stomachs. Certainly, God wants them fed. If the reign of God means anything at all to us, it means a sufficiency of food for all God's children. Why else would we pray in the Lord's Prayer that the kingdom come and in the next breath that we be granted daily bread? How can the coming of the reign of God *not* mean bread enough for all?

Yet we cannot feed the hungry of the world. We work to feed our own families. Most of us produce enough and to spare; we have some surplus. But we don't have enough left over to feed everyone in the world. If all the Christians in the world were to share what they could spare, would the hungry of the world be fed? Not likely. Nor is there a scheme or system lying close to hand that would ensure sufficient food for all. Socialism will not do it; capitalism will not do it; free enterprise will not do it. Neither will population control, free trade, green revolutions or red revolutions—or any other plan, movement, legislation, or reform known to any of us.

If there is among us one who knows—or thinks he or she knows—how to feed all the hungry of the world, let that person first make a tree or travel a thousand miles in a single bound. Then we shall all believe that he or she can indeed feed the hungry! For there to be an ample, fair distribution of food to all the human family—that requires a quantum leap. And we live in a world that limits us to the sowing of seeds.

That does not mean we can do nothing about world hunger. Each has close to hand a number of small things that can be done. We can eat less. We can plant kitchen gardens. We can give food to hungry neighbors. We can work in a community food pantry or soup kitchen. We can donate money to Bread for the World or to our denomination's Hunger Program. We can write to our representatives in Congress, urging support of legislation favorable to feeding the Third World. But for most of us, these small things are the most we can do.

Not to do these things—or to despise them for being too small to merit our attention—is to be unfaithful workers. Christian fidelity does not consist of sweeping gestures or grand schemes. It consists of the willing, cheerful acceptance of small tasks that lie close to hand. The insignificant things we do today may flower tomorrow into peace and justice for all. Surely in every work situation there are some things, however small, that you and I can do to advance the cause of God's kingdom.

A man who had a profound effect upon my career never knew that he did anything out of the ordinary. When I was near the final year at the theological seminary, I was treading water in a sea of possibilities. I didn't know what I wanted to do when I graduated: be a pastor, a teacher, a missionary, or a campus worker. One day the vice-president of the school met me on campus. He asked about my plans for the future. I told him that I couldn't make up my mind. "Don't just drift into something," he said, "and then say it was the will of God." Then he walked on by. What to him was a casual remark was to me like a clap of thunder. His words gave me no peace until I got my life into gear and made a clear decision.

Of such small, ordinary daily works is the life of Christian faithfulness made up. The great issues of our time—peace, hunger, race, nuclear holocaust, liberation—make it difficult for any of us to feel that there is much we can do. We are greatly tempted to drift and daydream. But near at hand, as close as our daily work, is a field in which we may sow small seeds. There is never "nothing to be done about it." God always allows us some small thing that we can do: write a letter, befriend a stranger, encourage a friend in despair, do our daily chores. Of such tiny seeds God can make great shrubs. Of such small beginnings the kingdom is made.

8

SUCCESS
The Parable
of the Secretly Growing Seed

The kingdom of God comes even as we sleep; its advent requires neither our wakefulness nor our watching. Even if we, like children hoping to see Santa fill the stockings, were to remain awake and on watch, we would not witness the advance of God's reign. For the process by which the better future develops is a hidden one. Jesus taught:

> The kingdom of God is as if a man should scatter seed upon the ground, and should sleep and rise night and day, and the seed should sprout and grow, he knows not how. The earth produces of itself, first the blade, then the ear, then the full grain in the ear. But when the grain is ripe, at once he puts in the sickle, because the harvest has come.
>
> (Mark 4:26–29)

God's ways of working are concealed from us. Just as the prescientific farmer knew nothing of the cellular process by which seeds develop into plants, so we—for all our science—know nothing of the inner workings of God's reign. Albert Einstein, the great theoretical physicist, sought all his life for a unified field theory that would combine, in one coherent pattern, all the various understandings of the laws of nature. He died without having found it. We also lack a comprehensive theory for explaining the work of God. We walk by faith, not by sight.

Oh, we know the *ends* to which God's activity is directed. As the farmer in Jesus' Parable of the Secretly Growing Seed knew to harvest the ripe grain, so we are prepared to rejoice in the triumph of peace over war, liberation over oppression, life over death. But we do not know with surety how these conditions come to pass. Nor do we know the month, day, or hour of their coming.

Progress an Illusion

Certainly we detect here and there evidence of the advance of the reign of God: Smallpox is eradicated; nations sign peace treaties; women escape the bondage of stereotypes. These triumphs, however, are more like the early buds that herald the coming of spring than they are like milestones that mark measured progress. They are signs that point in the direction we are headed; they are not laps completed in a race. Our great cities, in many ways triumphs of the arts and law and science, are never to be confused with the City of God. Rather we are like Abraham, of whom the author of Hebrews said, "He looked forward to the city which has foundations, whose builder and maker is God" (Heb. 11:10).

If we accept the Parable of the Secretly Growing Seed as a metaphor of human history, then progress on any measurable scale is an illusion. We can look back over the way humankind has come and may think to see movement of miles, yards, or even inches up an inclined plane. We may suppose that our struggles have lifted us above the level of those who lived before us. But is the twentieth century more peaceful, more humane, more just than the tenth, or even the first? We can testify to signs of a ripening civilization. We can point to evidence that a harvest is to be expected. But progress in any absolute sense is nothing of which we may boast.

In sum, we are not those who push heavy burdens up a road that leads ever higher. That is a heroic image of humankind. However, it is more Stoic than Christian. Rather, we are like those who scatter seeds on plowed earth and sleep and rise, sleep and rise, while the seeds grow to harvest—we know not how. That is the point of Jesus' Parable of the Secretly Growing Seed.

Scatterers of Seeds

The point was made in the previous chapter—and bears repeating—that it is no disgrace to be a scatterer of seeds. Consider the work of the Israelite prophets of the eighth century B.C.E., of whom Hosea is representative. What did Hosea do, other than scatter seeds? He lived in a time of relative peace and prosperity. Israel enjoyed a rest from the harassment of larger neighbors. But in spite of domestic tranquillity and economic abundance, Israel was in deadly danger. For like many people today, the Israelites could not stand prosperity. It made them anxious. They could not hold it with open hands; they became grasping. To ensure against the loss of their abundance, they turned to the cults.

In the eighth century B.C.E., Israel had a flirtation going with the cults of Baal. Baalism was the religion of the Canaanites, with whom Israel shared the land of Palestine. The cults of Baal were fertility cults. The Canaanites

did not leave to chance or to natural processes the birthing of lambs or the ripening of grain. To ensure good
harvests, they made lavish sacrifices to the Baals— fertility gods and goddesses. Instead of lying down at night in
restful sleep, leaving their harvest in the hands of a faithful God, they lay down at their altars with cult prostitutes.

The Israelites, nervous about their new prosperity,
could not resist being drawn into the cults of Baal. Why
take a chance? Why risk offending the local deities? If the
religion of Yahweh was good, why wasn't more religion
better? And so to the worship of Yahweh the Israelites
added the worship of the Baals. They made sacrifices and
joined in the sexually based worship.

To Hosea it was clear that this seduction by Baalism
meant the death of faith in Yahweh and the destruction of
Israel. But what could he do? As modern folk have
learned, the pull of a cult religion is very powerful. And
especially to people who want to believe in a god or gods
who exist only to guarantee prosperity. Hosea did what
he could: He publically denounced the worship of the
Baals and warned Israel that the nation would most certainly go under.

But what is one voice against a cultural tide? A friend,
hearing Hosea preaching in the streets, might well have
said to him, "Dear friend, you waste your time! You are
like one who scatters seed on rocky ground. What can
come of this obsession with the worship of Yahweh?"

Much came of it. The prophetic movement, of which
Hosea and Amos and their kind were essential parts, was
the salt that preserved Israel. Jesus of Nazareth as the
Messiah of Israel is unthinkable apart from the prophetic
movement. Hosea and the other prophets scattered seeds;
a harvest out of all proportion to their work was the

result. We would change the metaphor and say that they kept the ground plowed and fertile until Jesus—God's Good Seed—could be planted and grow to a harvest. When Jesus began his ministry, he followed the example of the prophets; he was a sower of seeds. He did not begin an organized political movement. Instead, he gathered around him a few like-minded disciples and taught them his understanding of the advent of God's kingdom. Then he sent them out to be the salt of the earth. Jesus preached a universal kingdom of peace and justice. But all he did to inaugurate it was to select a handful of the faithful and scatter them, as it were, to the four winds.

And since the time of Jesus, that is the way the kingdom has continued its advance. While we sleep and rise, sleep and rise, the kingdom grows and develops toward a great harvest. We may believe in the sowing; we may believe in the harvest. But the process by which the one becomes the other, we cannot see.

The Assembly Line

In this book, we want to show that the workers in Jesus' parables often serve as models for our work. But the Parable of the Secretly Growing Seed strains the imagination. What can a farmer in remote Palestine have in common, say, with an assembly-line worker at Ford or General Motors in Detroit?

The two are not so far apart as might first appear. Like the farmer, the assembly-line worker performs a task that is insignificant when measured against the final product. The worker at Ford or G.M. bolts the right front wheel to a Mustang or a Citation. But that worker cannot say at the end of eight hours, "I built a car today!" Even if he or she

drops out of the line and does not do the appointed bolt-
ing, someone else will do the job. There is about as much
connection between the Detroit worker's activity and the
finished automobile as there is between a handful of grain
tossed on the ground and a bushel of harvested wheat.
Both tasks are purposeful; both look to a finished product;
neither is a random activity. But no matter how much the
worker on the assembly line wants to do well or is devot-
ed to the job at hand, he or she cannot build a fine car.
The worker on the line can do only a small piece of the
assembly and hope that the finished product bears the
marks of excellence. It is reassuring to the consumer to be
told, "Nobody sweats the details like G.M." or "At Ford,
quality is Job 1." But the worker—doing his or her small
bit—cannot guarantee the final results.

Somewhat like the farmer, who must trust not only to
the hidden processes of growth but also must hope for
good weather, so the assembly-line worker is not part of a
foolproof system. We like to point to the worker on the
line as evidence that we moderns understand work and
have made it rational. We say that the assembly-line
worker is the ultimate symbol of a perfectly organized
work force. Each person does one small task, does it exactly the same way each time, and in the long run this is
bound to be the most productive way to parcel out labor.

But if anyone thinks that we have reduced productivity
to an exact science, then let that person explain why the
larger economic system—of which the assembly line is a
part as well as a symbol—is so often out of whack! Why
do we suffer from inflation, recession, unfair distribution
of both work and rewards? Why do we suffer from all
those other recurring economic ailments that keep us
from being at peace with our prosperity?

We are no better able to sleep at night than the first-century farmer, who had to worry about drought, insects, plant diseases, weeds, and thieves! The notion of the assembly-line worker—or the office worker—as a cog in a finely tuned machine is an illusion. It is as much an illusion as the notion of history as absolute progress.

True, the assembly line has led to general prosperity. But it is also true that we are as nervous about our production and reward system as were the Israelites of Hosea's time about their prosperity. Why else are we so greatly tempted by the modern cults of Baal? We will listen openmouthed to anyone who announces in a clear, well-modulated voice that he or she understands how the system works and will teach us the "secrets of success." One will sell us success in a book, another in a training course. Another will use the images of the rich and famous to entice us to buy certain clothes or drive a certain car—always with the inference that the purchase will join us to the truly successful. The cult of Baal had nothing on us; daily we make our sacrifices to the goddess Success.

If we can believe the Parable of the Secretly Growing Seed, the Scriptures know nothing of "secrets of success." Such secrets are hidden from us as surely as the process by which grain develops from seed to ear was hidden from the farmer in Jesus' parable. The God of history is a hidden God; no one knows how or when or by what steps the reign of God comes to fruition among us.

Who knows for sure why one person succeeds and another fails? If there is indeed such a thing as "success," it may be only an optical illusion! It is a matter of genes, luck, glands, sweat, geography, timing, and friends in the right places—and God alone knows what else or in what combination. Faithful workers learn to close their ears to seductive voices that promise to teach or sell the "secrets of success"; they know such secrets are hidden from us.

The Sleeper

The faithful worker is the one who lies down to sleep at night, confident that the fruits of human labor are in the hands of God. In Hosea's time the faithful Israelite could leave the birthing of lambs and the growth of wheat to the care and keeping of Yahweh. And the faithful worker today is the one who can leave success—as well as the workings of the divine kingdom—in the keeping of God.

Sleep, rest, confidence in the future—these are the true friends of faithful work—although that is *not* what we were taught as children! We were cautioned that only as we rose early and worked late, burning the midnight oil, would we get our share and maybe a wee bit more. When Russell Baker was a little boy, as he tells us in *Growing Up,* his mother feared that he lacked "gumption." How could Buddy amount to anything, she wondered out loud, if he didn't want to get out in the world and earn money? When he was eight, she set him to selling magazines and then newspapers. Once, when he showed a lack of spirit in hawking his papers, she snatched them from him and went out into the street, bawling, "Extra! Extra!" Now that's gumption! And that's what we children were told was needed to get on in this world.

But one learns over the years to resist the impulse to sacrifice play and sleep and leisure to work. One also learns to suspect the good intentions—and the future sanity—of anyone who works too hard. The Parable of the

5

FAIRNESS
The Parable of Workers in the Vineyard

Manhattan or Florida might serve as modern settings for Jesus' Parable of the Workers in the Vineyard. The scene is a shape-up; day laborers are gathered to be sent into the vineyards. It is reminiscent of a hiring hall near the docks, where stevedores wait to be formed into crews to unload ships, or of the tailgate of a truck in a citrus grove, where migrants cluster, hoping to be chosen to pick oranges. Jesus said:

For the kingdom of heaven is like a householder who went out early in the morning to hire laborers for his vineyard. After agreeing with the laborers for a denarius a day, he sent them into his vineyard. And going out about the third hour he saw others standing idle in the market place; and to them he said, "You go into the vineyard too, and whatever is right I will give you." So they went. Going out again about the sixth hour and the ninth hour, he did the same. And about the eleventh hour he went out and found others standing; and he said to them, "Why do you stand here idle all day?" They said to him, "Because no one has hired us." He said to them, "You go into the vineyard too." And when evening came, the

Secretly Growing Seed reminds us that it is not the tireless, restless worker who is the model of faithfulness. It is the one who sows the seed and trusts the promise.

A friend of mine once moved to a larger city, where his two children enrolled in the high school. Not long after the move, word came to him from the school guidance counselor that both his son and daughter were "overachievers." How could that be? he asked me in some bewilderment and amusement. How is it possible for kids to be *too* ambitious? Many of us who have worked with high school students could have told him about the superworker syndrome. In every high school generation there are a few highly talented and motivated kids who try to do everything. They have an abundance of natural ability; their motto is, "If I can, I must." They play on the teams, run for office, fiddle in the school orchestra, get good grades, go to dances, date, run the youth fellowships at their churches—and have time to give speeches on Americanism at Rotary Club luncheons! As Edna St. Vincent Millay wrote, "My candle burns at both ends; It will not last the night . . ."

Certainly that kind of hyperactivity is *not* what Jesus meant when he told his friends that they were to be lights in the world. If we have rightly understood the Parable of the Secretly Growing Seed, the image Jesus had of good work was more like that of sowing seed and trusting the promise. It is not possible, by taking thought or staying up late, to hurry the harvest. Neither is it possible, by burning the candle at both ends, to enlighten the world.

9
PATIENCE
The Parable
of the Wheat and the Weeds

A cruel presumption is punctured by Jesus' Parable of the Wheat and the Weeds. The presumption is this: The higher we aim, the more surely we are to bag rewards. We send children off to school, daughters off to work, and sons off to war with the same injunction: "Now do your best!" The unspoken promise is that the best pays off better. Our Puritan heritage has taught us that if we will mix virtue with elbow grease, our cup will overflow.

The presumption is false, and cruelly misleading, because it is contradicted by God's own experience in our world. As the Parable of the Wheat and the Weeds teaches, God's work evokes active opposition. God must be patient and wait until a time of harvest to gather anticipated rewards. And if we will work the works of God, why should we expect anything different for ourselves?

An Enemy in the Night

Jesus compared the kingdom of God to a farmer who sowed good seed, only to have an enemy come in the night and sow weeds in the same field.

> The kingdom of heaven may be compared to a man who sowed good seed in his field; but while men

> were sleeping, his enemy came and sowed weeds among the wheat, and went away. So when the plants came up and bore grain, then the weeds appeared also. And the servants of the householder came and said to him, "Sir, did you not sow good seed in your field? How then has it weeds?" He said to them, "An enemy has done this." The servants said to him, "Then do you want us to go and gather them?" But he said, "No; lest in gathering the weeds you root up the wheat along with them. Let both grow together until the harvest; and at harvest time I will tell the reapers, Gather the weeds first and bind them in bundles to be burned, but gather the wheat into my barn."
>
> (Matthew 13:24–30)

As we have noted before, it is usually not a wise strategy to treat Jesus' parables as allegories. (See chapter 1.) In the history of biblical interpretation, the allegorizing of Jesus' parables has led to much mischief. However, in the case of the Parable of the Wheat and the Weeds, the author has himself provided us with an allegorical interpretation. So just this once we have permission to read the parable as an allegory.

The author of the Gospel describes Jesus as explaining to his friends the Parable of the Wheat and the Weeds in this fashion:

> He who sows the good seed is the Son of man; the field is the world, and the good seed means the sons of the kingdom; the weeds are the sons of the evil

> one, and the enemy who sowed them is the devil;
> the harvest is the close of the age, and the reapers
> are angels.
>
> (Matthew 13:37–39)

When read as an allegory, our parable becomes a re-
prise of the entire biblical story, which also began in a
garden and which promises to end with a harvest. In the
beginning, the book of Genesis tells us, God set out to
plant righteousness on earth. But right away the divine
intent encountered opposition: Sin entered the scene; the
first humans were thrust out of the garden; the time of
God's patience began. At the end of the story is a Final
Judgment, in which good will be separated from evil, the
harm done to God's plan will be rectified, and the original
intention of God will be fully and finally realized.

It would not be accurate to say that in biblical history
two realms or kingdoms struggle for supremacy, the
realm of goodness and the realm of evil. The Bible knows
only one kingdom: the reign of God and God's righteousness. But the Bible is aware of a shadowy counter-king-
dom, a constant threat to the plans and purposes of God, a
potential for evil and disaster that from time to time is
manifest in the very midst of God's people and activity.
Sometimes this shadow kingdom is personified as the evil
one or the devil. Sometimes, as in the Book of Job, the
evil one is seen as the tempter, who is allowed by God to
test—though not to destroy—the faithful. The devil—Satan—is usually a reactive, not an active, force:
tempting the faithful to stray, making counteroffers. Like
the serpent in the Garden of Eden, the evil one insinuates
that what God has said may not be straightforward. Like
the tempter of Jesus in the desert, the evil one can quote

Scripture and, like the enemy in the Parable of the Wheat and the Weeds, has no strategy except to make trouble for the faithful and adulterate what is good and wholesome.

In the biblical story, the opposition of this evil one comes to a climax in the life of Jesus. In the Gospel narrative, Jesus is the good seed, the child of God sent into this world to become the first of many sisters and brothers. But the presence in the world of God's child evokes the very worst in humankind. Those institutions that ought to serve God's plan become perverse and destructive; the church, the state, the forces of law and order—even the popular will—turn on Jesus to do him in. Instead of being dikes against the chaos that is always imminent in human affairs, these institutions become the agents of chaos.

As we read the life of Jesus in the Gospels, we are amazed at the behavior of the scribes and Pharisees, Judas, Pontius Pilate, and the common folk who shout for Jesus' crucifixion. How is this possible? we wonder. Wasn't the goodness of Jesus apparent to all? How could they fail to see that they were killing the best man who ever lived? Like the servants in the Parable of the Wheat and the Weeds, who come in astonishment to their master and say, "Did you not sow good seed in the field?" so are we wonder-struck. It seems to us as though the opposition to Jesus sprang from nowhere, that it had neither reason nor rhyme, that it was wholly groundless. But there it was. As the householder said to his farmhands, "An enemy has done this." We should be reminded by his words of the fierce opposition to God's will and work that in the scriptural story surfaces time and time again.

Knowing the scriptural story, we should not be surprised at the turn taken in the Parable of the Wheat and the Weeds. As soon as we hear the words, "The kingdom of heaven may be compared to a man who sowed *good* seed in his field," we should suspect that something nasty is going to intervene before the day of harvest. Throughout history God's work has evoked active opposition. Didn't Jesus warn us of this? He said, "If any man would come after me, let him deny himself and take up his cross and follow me" (Matt. 16:24). The cross that Christians are to carry is the sure and certain opposition that they will encounter in this world if they attempt to follow the example of Jesus. Like master, so servants.

The Workplace No Different

The Parable of the Wheat and the Weeds describes what happened in one farmer's field. What happens in our fields of work is not all that different. Those of us who have tried to make our workplaces be small parts of God's larger plan know all too well what happens: We evoke active, fierce opposition. If you try to sow peace and justice in the field where you work, watch out! Once in an army barracks I stepped between two of my friends who had gotten into a fight. For my attempt to make peace, I got lumps on the head and bitter words. My experiences in trying to make the workplace a more just and humane place have not been so very different. Those who are content to watch for the biweekly check and the advent of Friday afternoon, who are content to feed their faces and their families—such people may go through a lifetime at work with little hassle. But those who try to make the workplace into something more nearly resembling the kingdom of God had better watch out! By some strange chemistry, such attempts turn the otherwise peaceful workplace into a battleground. The forces of opposition spring up like quick-sprouting weeds, almost overnight. And the scenario of the Parable of the Wheat and the Weeds is played out once more.

This cannot be advanced as a general description of all workplaces and all work. But it can be testified to by any of us who have tried to make our workplaces more than just locations where one earns a living. Within the experience of any of us who have tried that, some of the following things have happened.

Did you ever try to organize your fellow workers for better pay or better working conditions? Then you know how otherwise beneficent managers can suddenly turn cold and hard. Did you ever propose to your corporation heads that the corporation ought to serve some useful social end, above and beyond simply making a profit for the shareholders? Then you have seen the face of naked greed suddenly and harshly uncovered. Did you, as a homemaker, ever try to lift the life-style of your family above the ordinary and routine? Did you try to introduce into the daily round such concepts as efficiency, thrift, moderation, energy saving, or income sharing? Then you know how swiftly a peaceful spouse and cherubic children can turn mulish and mean.

When you were in the army or worked on a factory crew, did you ever catch abuse for volunteering? For being an eager beaver? For working beyond quitting time or beyond self-imposed work quotas? Or did you ever set for your own work a higher standard, a vision of perfection? And did you discover what happens within our own private world of work when we try to be, in our own eyes, sowers of good seed? Even there the weeds of sloth, apathy, and cynicism can sprout overnight!

Something not at all nice happens when, in the workplace or the working life, there is introduced the concept of "ought." As in, "We ought to spend less money on ourselves so that the hungry of the world can have enough." Or, "This company ought to do more for its workers who are parents—like having a day-care center for small children." Or, "Those of us who are making high salaries ought to take a cut so that some of the people lower on the scale can get cost-of-living increases."

To such suggestions opposition quickly shows its head. And that opposition is more than just a natural resentment of eager beavers, show-offs, teacher's pets, and hustlers. It seems true of the workplace, as it is in the larger world, that when good seed is planted, choking weeds spring up to counter it.

What is true of virtue in the workplace is also often true of excellence. Let there be summoned to the stand as a witness anyone who has persisted in seeking excellence in an art, a craft, or a scientific discipline. That person will tell you that the world is *not* waiting breathlessly for a new style in painting, the discovery of a new star, or a new sound in music. When Stravinsky's ballet *The Rite of Spring* was first performed in Paris in 1913, music lovers rioted; the police had to restore order. Galileo's astronomical discoveries were actively opposed by church authorities; he had to deny his findings to escape excommunication. When you were a student, did you ever try to move beyond merely "getting by"? Did you seek total mastery of a subject? Then you know how the world treats ugly ducklings who yearn to be swans!

In the world of winners and hustlers and get-'em-tigers, it is commonplace to hear, "Look at the turtle. He gets somewhere only if he sticks his neck out." Right? Wrong!

A lot of adventuresome turtles end up in the soup. If you want to survive in the world of work, the best advice is *not* to stick your neck out. Rather, it is to build for yourself a protective shell and stay inside it. Try to excel and you'll encounter trouble.

A Model of Patience

Who, then, is the model for Christian faithfulness in the workplace? If workers who try to make the factory or office a more just and humane place get clobbered, what should we say to them? Don't do it? Do it anyway?

If the Parable of the Wheat and the Weeds suggests a model, it is the owner of the field—the farmer who waited patiently for the harvest to separate the good wheat from the weeds. When his servants came to him in anger and wanted to root out the weeds planted by his enemy, he advised patience. Like those servants, we are advised by the parable to exercise patience and restraint when we encounter opposition to good works. For, like the farmer, we know of an end time, a harvest, when the good will be separated from the evil, and all opposition to God's purposes will be thwarted. *The faithful Christian worker cultivates patience in the face of opposition to excellence or justice.*

The person who for me best exemplifies that patience is our sixteenth president, Abraham Lincoln. Of all our leaders he tried the least to evade or escape conflict; once the Civil War was joined, he did not try to live above the battle. He was our most "worldly" of presidents, the most earthy. His hands were as dirty with deals as any other politician's. His hands were bloodier than most. Yet in all that he did as our national leader, he did with that terrible patience of those who know that in the end God must be allowed to decide between good and evil, right and wrong. That long-suffering of Lincoln comes to full expression in his second inaugural address, delivered in the final stages of the War Between the States:

> Neither party expected for the war the magnitude or the duration which it has already attained. Neither anticipated that the *cause* of the conflict might cease with or even before the conflict itself should cease. Each looked for an easier triumph, and a result less fundamental and astounding. Both read the same Bible and pray to the same God, and each invokes His aid against the other. It may seem strange that any men should dare to ask a just God's assistance in wringing their bread from the sweat of other men's faces, but let us judge not, that we be not judged. The prayers of both could not be answered. That of neither has been answered fully.... With malice toward none, with charity for all, with firmness in the right as God gives us to see the right, let us strive on to finish the work we are in, to bind up the nation's wounds, to care for him who shall have borne the battle and for his widow and his orphan, to do all which may achieve and cherish a just and lasting peace among ourselves and with all nations.

From such a person we can learn to be patient. We can learn how to behave when we encounter fierce and determined resistance to good works. We can persist in sowing good seed and restrain ourselves from rooting out evil. We can be confident that a harvesttime has been appointed, when all matters will be dealt with in a fully satisfactory way.

A final word of caution: Patience in the face of opposition is not the same as tolerance for evil. The Parable of the Wheat and the Weeds does not suggest that we either ignore evil or pretend it does not exist. Rather, it suggests a strategy for dealing with resistance to goodness and excellence. Our task is not to meet wickedness head-on—as though by our efforts we could rid the workplace of sloth, greed, laziness, indifference, cruelty. Our task is to wait patiently for the time of harvest. That is a work any of us can do—pope, potter, clerk, cardinal, president, or pattern maker.

10
ENDOWMENTS
The Parable of the Talents

We see the present as linked to the future by promises; God sees that linkage as investments. We look for the world to become more just, more peaceful, more humane; God looks for endowments to show a profit. That is the teaching of the Parable of the Talents, Jesus' story of the man who entrusted his money to his servants and then went away on a long journey.

> For it will be as when a man going on a journey called his servants and entrusted to them his property; to one he gave five talents, to another two, to another one, to each according to his ability. Then he went away. He who had received the five talents went at once and traded with them; and he made five talents more. So also, he who had the two talents made two talents more. But he who had received the one talent went and dug in the ground and hid his master's money. Now after a long time the master of those servants came and settled accounts with them. And he who had received the five talents came forward, bringing five talents more, saying, "Master, you delivered to me five talents; here I have made five talents more." His master said

to him, "Well done, good and faithful servant; you have been faithful over a little, I will set you over much; enter into the joy of your master." And he also who had the two talents came forward, saying, "Master, you delivered to me two talents; here I have made two talents more." His master said to him, "Well done, good and faithful servant; you have been faithful over a little, I will set you over much; enter into the joy of your master." He also who had received the one talent came forward, saying, "Master, I knew you to be a hard man, reaping where you did not sow, and gathering where you did not winnow; so I was afraid, and I went and hid your talent in the ground. Here you have what is yours." But his master answered him, "You wicked and slothful servant! You knew that I reap where I have not sowed, and gather where I have not winnowed? Then you ought to have invested my money with the bankers, and at my coming I should have received what was my own with interest. So take the talent from him, and give it to him who has the ten talents. For to every one who has will more be given, and he will have abundance; but from him who has not, even what he has will be taken away. And cast the worthless servant into the outer darkness; there men will weep and gnash their teeth."

(Matthew 25:14–30)

Like the master in the Parable of the Talents, God has great expectations. The kingdom of God is among us in the form of divine investments.

We cannot say with certainty what those investments are. We should be fools to try. For in the parable one servant hides the money entrusted to him in the ground, saying that he knows the master to be a hard man. But when the master returns, that servant is punished. We should be alerted by his example and not trust too much in our own knowledge of the Master.

But we can make some educated guesses about the nature of God's investments in the present. In Jesus' day a talent was a fixed sum of money. We can say that the money in the parable represents the gospel. For surely God does not intend that the good news of reconciliation be hoarded. Rather, God wants it to be shared as widely as possible. The book of Acts describes the gift of God's Spirit to the church as being followed by a great expansion of the Christian fellowship throughout the world. The good news is for giving away, not for storing away. To paraphrase a popular statement, "The church lives by sharing the gospel as fire lives by burning."

Fair enough. The history of the church is littered with the wrecks of institutions that simply treasured the gospel of Jesus Christ and were afraid to share it widely. In the frontier days of America, Presbyterianism nearly painted itself into a corner; it decided not to organize new congregations faster than they could be supplied with fully trained pastors. But the Methodists felt no such constraint. They sent out circuit riders, who scattered the gospel—and new congregations—like Johnny Appleseed his cores. The Methodists won the West for Jesus.

Others would see represented in the money in the parable the faith that God has entrusted to us during the time of Christ's physical absence. Indeed, the New Testament tells us that faith in Christ is God's gift; it tells us also of the fruits (profits) that God expects to issue from that gift:

love, joy, peace, patience, kindness, goodness, faithfulness, gentleness, self-control (cf. Gal. 5:22–23).

Sad to say, faith—like the gospel—has been hoarded both by individual believers and by Christian groups. Some believers will not allow a single word or gesture in the traditional liturgy—the service of public worship —to be changed, for fear that somehow the true faith might not be expressed or handed on. And then they wonder why no new believers are attracted to their fellowship! Against just such a mind-set, which regards religious tradition as an inviolate trust, John the Baptist railed. "Bear fruit that befits repentance," he shouted at those who came to hear him preach, "and do not presume to say to yourselves, 'We have Abraham as our father'; for I tell you, God is able from these stones to raise up children to Abraham. Even now the axe is laid to the root of the trees; every tree therefore that does not bear good fruit is cut down and thrown into the fire" (Matt. 3:8–10).

So the talents in Jesus' parable may represent the gospel, they may represent faith, or—to follow the popular interpretation—they may represent God-given abilities. Our English word "talent" translates a word that in the original story meant a large sum of money. Because of the popularity of this parable, the word "talent" has come to mean, by analogy, "abilities." And there is biblical warrant for that. The New Testament tells of abilities—gifts—that God gives to some in the church and not to all: prophecy, healing, working miracles, speaking in tongues, teaching.

But when such gifts are regarded as having value in and of themselves, or as investing their recipients with privilege, they turn into liabilities. For example, the great temptation of those who receive the gift of ecstatic speech is to regard "speaking in tongues" as the sure proof of divine election. Such pride precedes a great fall. Evidently speaking in tongues was widely practiced in the congregation in Corinth in the time of Paul. In order to curb the practice, Paul would let at most three persons speak in tongues in a public meeting; then he insisted that someone translate such sounds into edifying speech. For otherwise, he argued, it would be as though the divine gift had been hoarded and had brought no benefit to the entire church.

In sum, the money in the Parable of the Talents may represent the gospel, faith in Christ, or God-given abilities. A useful way of referring to all these without singling out any for preferential treatment is to call them "endowments." For endowments may be trusts, gifts, abilities, or even sums of money.

We do well to avoid disputation over the precise meaning for us of the talents in the parable. For in such disputes we let ourselves be diverted from the main thrust of the story, which is this: The better future is linked to the present through God's endowments. And there is a corollary to that main teaching, which is: The future will be harsh on those whose endowments show no profit. God expects a return on investments!

As we have seen earlier in this book, Jesus' view of history is not like that which prevails today. We moderns tend to think of history in terms of progress, of a rising tide that will lift all boats. Not so, implies the Parable of the Talents. Some will be rewarded at the Last Judgment; some will be punished—according to their faithfulness in the employment of their endowments.

What Else Is New?

So what else is new? This notion of history may not square with our ideas of progress, but it certainly squares with what we know about the workplace. There, as in Jesus' parable, workers with unequal endowments are rewarded or penalized according to whether or not their work shows a profit for their masters.

In our workplaces, there are five-talent, three-talent, and one-talent workers. In the public schools there are superintendents, teachers, and janitors. A pro-football team has owners, quarterbacks, linemen, and taxi-squad members. There are corporation presidents, middle managers, and clerks. And the president gets a whopping salary compared to the hardest-working clerk.

Some think that the arrangement of rewards is all wrong. They think that the workplace ought to be ruled as a democracy both as to endowments and rewards. Each worker should enjoy equal opportunity; each should be paid the same salary. Such people see the company janitor, given the same opportunities as the president, equally capable of filling the top job. Well, a cat may look at a king and a janitor may dream of a president's salary, but a dream it will remain. The workplace knows no democracy either of endowments or of rewards; it knows only a hierarchy of both. To those few holding the top jobs, it pays huge rewards. And it pays minimal wages to the many with menial jobs. And to those at the entry level of employment, as to the one-talent man in Jesus' parable, the workplace is merciless in its punishments for non-performance.

Minorities that press for job quotas on the grounds of prior denial of opportunity are swimming against a powerful current. The workplace seems to reach out instinctively to embrace those with the greater endowments, offering them even more; and from those who have few endowments, it tends to remove what little has been given.

The poor wretch in the parable who is punished for hoarding his small investment is a distorted yet recognizable mirror image of the unskilled worker in our society. For if such workers do not make the very most of their limited gifts, even these gifts will be rejected by the economy. The unemployment rolls are not crowded with the names of the gifted—Rhodes scholars, class valedictorians, neurosurgeons. But those rolls are full of the names of those with few skills, limited energy, low esteem. One could think that Jesus had just visited a state unemployment office when he said "But from him who has not, even what he has will be taken away" (Matt. 25:29).

Is There a Pattern?

Must we then conclude that the teaching of the Parable of the Talents is wholly negative? Can we extract from it no pattern for the faithful Christian worker? We can, but only if we first look carefully and soberly at its portrait of the faithless worker.

All too prevalent in our society is the attitude of that person who makes a virtue of what the parable labels a vice: that is, sitting on one's endowments. In the Broadway musical *She Loves Me*, a middle-aged clerk sings to his young friend:

> Actually, my creed is short and simple,
> Do not lose your job.

That voice is one in a vast chorus. How often have you heard it? How often have you been stonewalled in a government agency or a department store by a clerk who says, "I'd like to help you, but I don't want to lose my job." The creed is nearly universal!

What is the flip side of that record? It is the song of the worker who is not afraid to put his or her endowments at risk. The one who dares to invest even meager endowments in a better future—that is the faithful worker.

In the Parable of the Talents, the profits on investments are revealed only when the master returns after a long absence. And it is only with the wisdom of hindsight that we can point to the truly faithful Christian worker. In the last century, many Americans went abroad as missionaries of the gospel. No doubt the family and friends of many said of them, "Poor Grace and George! Going off to bury their talents in some God-forsaken native village. And they could have amounted to something here at home." Today, even George and Grace might be astounded to return to life and witness the modern miracle of a worldwide church, much of it the product of the nineteenth-century missionary movement.

Even with such hindsight, we surely will be blind to most of the profits on God's investments if we look only to those fields that society regards as most promising: medicine, astrophysics, computer science, the arts and letters. Or if we let our eyes be dazzled with the brilliance of those with multiple endowments: Nobel laureates, Pulitzer Prize winners, senators, home-run hitters, millionaires. For the Parable of the Talents suggests that each of us, no matter how few our gifts, represents an investment in God's better future. Appearing on the *Tonight Show*, Sam Levenson quoted a rabbinic saying: "Every child born into the world has a message to deliver." That is the essence of the Parable of the Talents. It is a summons to all workers to make the most of their limited gifts—to put at risk what they have been given, in the confidence that it may yield dividends.

Three Examples

In recent years the mass media have brought to public attention three persons who exemplify what can happen when a one-talent worker is not afraid to gamble on the future. One is the British animal behaviorist Jane Goodall, who has spent her adult life in the jungles of Africa, observing and recording the activities of chimps. Another is the Mississippi novelist and short-story writer Eudora Welty, who has spent a lifetime recording the folkways of her small-town neighbors. The third is the Yugoslavian nun Mother Teresa, who has given her life to the destitute of India.

As we learn about their careers and watch these women being interviewed on TV talk shows, several things strike us about all three. All are much like the ordinary folk in our own families and neighborhoods. Eudora Welty could be a favorite aunt; Jane Goodall, the cousin who loved animals; Mother Teresa, the Sunday school teacher we had in the fourth grade. As human beings, they are so ordinary, so accessible.

As we watch them, we think: I could have done those things if I had wanted to badly enough. Each has taken a modest endowment—a gift for observation, a talent for patient watching, a capacity for physical caring—and made it yield large returns. And their gifts are not rare. Some of them we can recognize as being like our own.

What is most remarkable about these women is that they lack the talent for self-promotion that we are accustomed to see in so-called "great" men and women. They seem to know quite well that they are not ten-talent people. They are modest about their endowments. And yet we recognize that their contributions to the kingdom of God are not insignificant.

To take one gift, one special interest, and to work with it and at it modestly, selflessly, with no need for self-promotion or thought of becoming "great," that is the pattern the Parable of the Talents suggests to us.

We shrink from that teaching; it implies high risk. We know all too well the fear of the faithless one-talent worker who hid his money in the ground. So each of us has been given a message to deliver. What if we garble the words? What if we misplace our endowments? What if we have set our hearts on Washington, D.C., but the action for us is in Waterloo, Iowa? What if that itch in our fingers for the frets of a guitar is really more appropriate to the handle of a hammer? The less our endowments, the more we are haunted by the question, *What if we fail?*

Certainly there is risk in trusting that our endowments are God's investments in the better future. The savings and loan account guarantees five and a half percent on a savings account, with the federal government standing surety behind it. But standing behind God there is no one who will bail us out if we are wrong about our choices. However, the Parable of the Talents points us to an even greater danger: doing nothing with what we have been given. The odds favor those who take the plunge; the better future is on the side of those who invest themselves fully in the present.

God trusts us more than we trust ourselves. That is the bottom line. God's future belongs to those who, more than they treasure security, cherish a hope that someday they may hear, "Well done, good and faithful servant; . . . enter into the joy of your master" (Matt. 25:23).

11
ACCOUNTABILITY
The Parable of the Dishonest Steward

The better future that Jesus announced and inaugurated is not a paradise for fools. God's reign brings a reckoning. To those who persist in willful ignorance, the kingdom comes as a rude surprise. That is the clear teaching of Jesus' Parable of the Dishonest Steward.

There was a rich man who had a steward, and charges were brought to him that this man was wasting his goods. And he called him and said to him, "What is this that I hear about you? Turn in the account of your stewardship, for you can no longer be steward." And the steward said to himself, "What shall I do, since my master is taking the stewardship away from me? I am not strong enough to dig, and I am ashamed to beg. I have decided what to do, so that people may receive me into their houses when I am put out of the stewardship." So, summoning his master's debtors one by one, he said to the first, "How much do you owe my master?" He said, "A hundred measures of oil." And he said to him, "Take your bill, and sit down quickly and write fifty." Then he said to another, "And how much do you owe?" He said, "A hundred measures of wheat." He said to him, "Take your bill, and write eighty." The master commended the dishonest steward for his shrewdness; for the sons of this world are more shrewd in dealing with their own generation than the sons of light.

(Luke 16:1–8)

We can fully appreciate the teaching of this parable if we yield to one temptation and resist another. Let us suspend moral judgment and give full license to our secret approval of white-collar crime. Many of us are privately pleased when someone diddles the tax man, mugs the corporation, or makes off with company property. When we all watched M°A°S°H, we were endlessly amused when Hawkeye tricked the supply sergeant out of a box of medicine or a case of Scotch—or a jeep. When we read in the *Times* that a bank teller has made off to Latin America with a bundle of the bank's money, we may secretly hope that the teller is never caught.

So let's hear it for the steward in the parable. He is a delight to the con artist, the grifter, the petty pilferer that lurks in each of us. Anyone who has shaved a few bucks from a Form 1040 has got to admire that steward. He beat the system! A hundred measures of oil is nearly nine hundred gallons. The steward could reasonably expect that his partners in crime would take care of him for a long, long time.

Although we yield to the temptation to admire the dishonest steward for his cleverness, we must resist the temptation to identify him as someone we ought to know. It would be tempting, for example, to say that Jesus had in mind the high priest of the Jerusalem cult. Had not Israel, entrusted with the promises and the law of God, been less than a faithful steward? Didn't Jesus say that the parable is directed against "the sons of light"? Who were these sons, if not the children of Israel? And were not the Jews driven from the city in 70 c.e., to live in poverty and misery in the diaspora? It is quite probable that Jesus told the Parable of the Dishonest Steward to pious Jews, who trusted that they were children of light and who believed in a wonderful day when God would intervene to vindicate them and punish their enemies.

However, as we learned earlier, to allegorize the parables of Jesus is to violate the accepted rules of interpretation. Most scholars agree that Jesus did not intend his parables as allegories; usually he had in mind one point only. And in this particular case, as Jesus himself makes clear, the point of the parable is not dependent on the identity of the steward. It is, rather, the action of the steward that is revelatory. He knew a day of accounting to be imminent; he took precautionary measures. He was shrewd. Would that the hearers in Jesus' day were so wise!

A Day of Reckoning

It is a wise man or woman who knows that the coming of the reign of God brings a reckoning. By his parable Jesus presents to humankind a warning: Take care that you do not act the fool. You know the will of God. Do not act as though you had forever to obey it. *Now* is the day of obedience. And if you do not know that, you are in for a rude surprise.

But this should come as no surprise to those who know the Scriptures. From beginning to end the Bible tells of the advent of a God who holds persons accountable. According to the creation story in the book of Genesis, God created humans and put them in the garden to till it—to care for it and to live from its bounty. Adam and Eve were stewards, a steward being one put in charge of the affairs of another with permission to enjoy the fruits of his or her labor—while remaining faithful to the initial charge. When Adam and Eve betrayed their stewardship by doing the one thing they were told not to do, they were put out of the garden.

Unlike the steward in Jesus' parable, Adam and Eve had no employer. Nor did they have the option of digging or begging. For them it was dig—or die! The man was set to wrest a living from the soil, with the woman as his reluctant helper. (Is it too much to say that all work, as we know it, is the consequence of a botched stewardship on the part of the earliest humans?)

What was true in the beginning remains true throughout the story of God's dealings with humankind. What the prophets said to Israel was, in effect, what God had said to Adam and Eve: I gave you all this to enjoy. Could you not have been faithful to my commands? God gave to Israel the promises and the commandments. Israel knew—or should have known—what God wanted. And yet such a mess was made of that stewardship! To those in eighth-century Israel who afflicted the poor, took bribes, and neglected the needy, Amos lashed out with these words:

> Woe to you who desire the day of the LORD!
>   Why would you have the day of the LORD?
> It is darkness, and not light;
>   as if a man fled from a lion,
>   and a bear met him;

or went into the house and leaned with his hand
    against the wall,
and a serpent bit him.
Is not the day of the LORD darkness, and not light,
    and gloom with no brightness in it?
(Amos 5:18–20)

A modern Amos, preaching to our religious Establishment, might be less poetic: "You think you are so smart!
You say that you know all about the coming of the Lord.
Don't you know that the Lord will expect, upon his coming, to find peace and justice on earth?" We would do
well to reflect that the prophecy of Amos to Israel was
borne out. Not long after Amos spoke his harsh words,
the nation of Israel—the Northern Kingdom—was carried off into slavery. A day of reckoning came all too soon.

The New Testament, like the Old, knows of a day of
reckoning. No one in all of Scripture was less disposed to
glorify work than the apostle Paul. Yet he could write to
his friends in Corinth, "For we must all appear before the
judgment seat of Christ, so that each one may receive
good or evil, according to what he has done in the body"
(2 Cor. 5:10).

Both Testaments announce in chorus that the reign of
God brings a day of reckoning. In telling the Parable of
the Dishonest Steward, Jesus was only reminding his
hearers of what they already knew: The Day of the Lord
will require each to give an accounting of his or her
stewardship.

The Accountability Factor

This is underscored if we read the parable from the standpoint of our own daily work. For each of us a day of reckoning hangs overhead. Accountability is an essential feature of work. No one labors purely for the work's sake, or for his or her own sake. Even if you don't have to look a time clock in the face, someone is watching you! Dagwood Bumstead has Mr. Dithers; Hawkeye has Colonel Potter; the President has the U.S. electorate; the spouse, as well as the children, waits for Father or Mother to come home. In some form or other, Big Brother or Big Mother watches over us all.

This "accountability factor" is a major source of stress in the workplace. It brings sweat to the brow of every Eve and every Adam wrestling to make the economy yield a living. One of the bitter struggles that will take place in the American workplace in this decade will be over "computer monitoring." Each of our nearly twenty million clerical workers may be faced with the prospect of each single motion being made at a computer keyboard, registered, added up, and measured against a fixed standard of performance for that particular job. That would seem to raise the accountability factor to an impossibly high degree.

Nevertheless, it is part of the nature of work that we are held accountable. It is not so much that if we do wrong, we will get our hand slapped. Rather, if we do not measure up, we will be given a less rewarding job. We had best do well at what we like best, or we will be given work that is less appealing. If we can't be honest and profitable stewards, there is always the beggar's bowl or the ditchdigger's shovel.

One of the prospects that makes retirement so attractive to many is the idea that as retirees they won't have to account to anyone for the use of their time. On the other hand, one of the hardest things about growing up is to have to accept the accountability factor built into work. Children know almost from the crib that if they do wrong they will be punished. But it is cruel to learn also that if you do not do well, you will be demoted.

In the TV series *The Adams Chronicles,* little John Quincy tells his father that he is tired of studying Latin; he says that he plans to be a farmer and sees no use for a dead language. His father obliges him by sending him out to dig a long ditch. When John Quincy comes in at the end of the day, worn to the nub, he asks his father, "Is there nothing in life but Latin or the ditch?" John Adams tells his son with some regret, "Johnny, I'm afraid not."

Those who will not grasp a pen must grab a shovel. There is nothing but Latin or the ditch. If you cannot do the one, you must do the other. Call to witness the steward in Jesus' parable. He knew that if he got fired from his job, he would have to beg or dig. No one would offer him a post similar to the one he was leaving—unless he took extraordinary measures. Not to know this, implies Jesus in his commentary on the steward's action, is to be a fool.

God's better future is not a paradise for fools. Rather, it is like the Garden of Eden, where Adam and Eve were set to till the garden and to care for it and enjoy its fruits. Not to know that we human beings are stewards of this earth and of its bounty is to lack essential wisdom. We are all accountable, and work is the sign and occasion of that accountability.

The inevitable accountability of work was brought home to me once in a strange way. I was taking a noontime walk in Riverside Park, across the street from my office building. I came upon a masterfully constructed limestone wall, on which was scrawled with paint from a spray can: IT's NOT MY FAULT! I could well imagine that a young malcontent had left that message for WASP Establishment types like me. But the very act indicted this graffiti artist: using a can of paint, itself intended for painting woodwork or furniture, to deface a lovely product of the stonemason's craft defaced in turn a place created to give work-weary men and women a bit of pleasure and leisure. We are all stewards, know it or not, like it or not.

The Steward

Although its teaching is couched in negative terms, the Parable of the Dishonest Steward has a positive message for us workers. If we heed Jesus' warning and ask in good faith, What shall we then do?, the parable itself has response for us. Our answer is the metaphor of the steward. *To see ourselves as stewards is to see our work as combining freedom and responsibility without loss of either.* It is a way of thinking about our labor that does not remove us one step from the real world but enables us to live in that world in a new and better way. And that is as true for corporate entities—businesses and industries—as it is for individuals.

What is a steward? In biblical times a steward was the man whom a rich landowner put over the affairs of his household and fields. The steward was more than a chief servant. He was responsible not only for the welfare of the other servants but also for the business affairs of the establishment. As the Parable of the Dishonest Steward tells us, he was free to manage the business of the master without day-by-day interference. So long as he was careful and prudent in his dealings, he had the complete confidence of his master and free reign over his master's property.

The image of the steward can be applied to groups or to individuals. In a real sense Israel was the steward of God's promises and commandments. It was to an entire people that God gave covenants and entrusted the law. Israel enjoyed a rare blend of freedom and responsibility, of election and mission. The apostle Paul took the metaphor of the steward and applied it to the church: "This is how one should regard us, as servants of Christ and stewards of the mysteries of God" (1 Cor. 4:1).

The steward image may be applied to modern business. The healthiest thing for a modern corporation might be to learn to think of itself as a steward of resources, both material and human. Such a self-image might free managers from thinking themselves bound hand and foot to serve their stockholders, no matter what harm was done the common good. One of the more pitiable sights of this decade has been a parade of corporate managers—and that includes union officials—trying to explain to the public why a giant industry has to abandon its mill in Youngstown (or Pittsburgh), say, leaving thousands of workers unemployed, a community hurting for tax revenues, and a whole area of the country stripped of an essential industry. What is most pitiable is to hear these managers say, "Our accountants have given us a grim picture. If we want to stay in business, we have to move our plant to Korea where labor is cheaper."

Fools! Why didn't they ask themselves earlier in the game: What is our responsibility to our work force? To the community? To the state of Ohio (or Pennsylvania) and the American public? How can we alter our methods of production, our wage scale, our facilities in order to be good stewards? Since they did not ask those questions, they have reaped a harvest of human misery and economic dislocation—even ruin. Had they regarded themselves as accountable to God—and not simply to their own accountants—they might have avoided their day of accounting.

It is easier to see the usefulness of the metaphor of the steward when it is applied to the work of the individual. It is particularly valuable in a situation where someone is forced to labor in an oppressive situation. Hear what the author of Ephesians could write to fellow Christians:

> Slaves, be obedient to those who are your earthly masters, with fear and trembling, in singleness of heart, as to Christ; . . . doing the will of God from the heart, rendering service with a good will as to the Lord and not to men, knowing that whatever good any one does, he will receive the same again from the Lord, whether he is a slave or free.
>
> (Ephesians 6:5–8)

In contemporary terms, the Ephesians passage might sound more like this: "So you are stuck in your job. Gotta work for a boss who is a real crumb. Can't quit, or the wife and kids might go hungry. Tell you what: Think of yourself as a free man. You belong to Jesus. Act like it! Do your work as though you were doing it for him, and not for your boss. Don't worry. There will come a day of reckoning. Everyone will get his! If you have done well, you'll hear about it. And those who have leaned on you—they'll get theirs!"

Future circumstance may force all of us—individuals and corporations—to choose the model of the steward for our work and for our life-styles. Remember the oil shortages of 1973 and 1979. Suddenly we realized how dependent is our highly organized economy on nonrenewable sources of energy. If we want to preserve our economy, we may have no choice but to exercise better stewardship of natural resources, ceasing to regard them as our private stock but as held in trust for our children and their children.

Do you remember something else about 1973 and 1979—how we as a nation pulled together to get out of a bind? We cut our highway speed; we carpooled; we converted oil burners to gas heaters; we insulated our attics; we put weather stripping around doors and windows; we took a hard look at solar energy. Those measures didn't add up to Jimmy Carter's "moral equivalent of war," but they gave a boost to our morale. Meaning was given to sacrifice. Once more the common good was a significant idea.

The model of the steward can be a liberating one in a world increasingly bureaucratized, where clerical workers are monitored by computers, where in many homes the personal computer—Little Brother—stares with a blank, accusing eye. We may be grateful for a model of work that proclaims at once our accountability to God and our freedom from absolute tyranny in the workplace.

12
SLEEPING
The Parable
of the Watchful Servants

God's kingdom knows neither clocks nor calendars. God's reign breaks in upon human affairs, not like an airplane landing on schedule, but like the master of a household, arriving home at the moment of his own choosing. That is the teaching of Jesus' Parable of the Watchful Servants.

Let your loins be girded and your lamps burning, and be like men who are waiting for their master to come home from the marriage feast, so that they may open to him at once when he comes and knocks. Blessed are those servants whom the master finds awake when he comes; truly, I say to you, he will gird himself and have them sit at table, and he will come and serve them. If he comes in the second watch, or in the third, and finds them so, blessed are those servants! But know this, that if the householder had known at what hour the thief was coming, he would not have left his house to be broken into. You also must be ready; for the Son of man is coming at an unexpected hour.

(Luke 12:35–40)

The Parable of the Watchful Servants is built on the imagery of an oriental householder who has gone off to a wedding banquet. He has told his servants to stay awake until his return and to unlock the door when he appears. There is no telling at what hour he will come; the feast, with its drinking and eating, may last well into the early morning hours. Those servants who are most likely to receive the master's commendation—and even special favors—are they who are awake, hear his knock, and open the door to him at once.

The clear implication of the parable is that the kingdom comes when God wills it, not according to any timetable that humans either devise or think to discern. Faithfulness consists in being awake and expectant of the coming of the kingdom; it sits easy to clocks and calendars. The faithful servant of God does not count minutes or hours. God's servants count it all-important that they be awake to the possibility of the Sovereign's coming at any moment.

This freedom from clocks and calendars is one of the distinguishing marks of God's reign. It keeps us from confusing God's realm with other powers, principalities, or ruling principles. Take, as an example, one of the basic assumptions of the twentieth century, the notion of progress. One could not find in modern thought an idea that rules with greater power and persuasiveness than the notion of progress. The imagery is that of humankind on a giant inclined plane; all change moves us slowly yet inevitably upward toward a time of greater development. We are better off than our forebears; our children will be better off than we are; our great-great-grandchildren will have things even better. We do not know how far the plane stretches into the future. (Some futurists paint scenarios of a time when human intellect will have evolved to the point where each human can know the thoughts of the other without the necessity of speech.) Nor do we have a timetable for progress. There is movement, but humankind moves at its own hidden pace. Looking back in retrospect, with such intellectual tools as the theory of evolution, we can point to advances, though we have no precise way of measuring these. Nonetheless, progress depends upon some kind of timetable, upon a future that is measurably better than the past. Progress gives the present pregnancy; most certainly the present contains the seeds of future goods and greatness.

A competing twentieth-century notion is the Marxist one of history as class struggle. In this ideology, history is a constant struggle between the haves and the have-nots. Marxism envisions a time when the struggle is won, when there will be no social classes. So it can tolerate, for the present, the injustices of a police state; it argues that such restraints will not be necessary in a classless society. For Marxism, time is everything. Present injustices are meaningful in terms of both past wrongs and future rights. The present is pregnant with the seeds of an assuredly better future.

The so-called "nature religions," by which millions have lived and many still live, have as their guiding imagery neither an inclined plane nor a class struggle. Their imagery is that of the wheel, turning on its axle. If the affairs of humans and their world are indeed "going somewhere," it is through the process of an endless turning of the wheel. In the spring, after winter's cold, comes seedtime; in the summer comes ripening; in the fall comes harvest; followed by winter, spring, summer, and fall again. Those whom we regard primitive peoples measured those cycles—the changes of the moon and stars and seasons—and built calendars and invented what we call "time." For them, the present was pregnant with meaning as a measurable place on the great wheel of the cycles of nature. Their future was more or less predictable in terms of the return of the full moon, the advent of colder weather, the migration of birds. The present had significance as the moment on the way to the time when the moon would again be full, when seedtime would come around again, the trees would blossom, or the sun begin once more to appear earlier and earlier in each day.

Not only are ruling principles conceived mainly in time-bound images; so are earthly kingdoms. We say of nations, empires, states, and civilizations that they are born, flourish, decay, die, and are reborn. None is thought of as eternal. Although Hitler boasted of a Thousand-Year Reich, it lasted less than two decades. In the words of Isaac Watts's hymn:

> Time, like an ever-rolling stream,
>   Bears all its sons away;
> They fly forgotten, as a dream
>   Dies at the opening day.

In sharp contrast to ruling principles, principalities, powers, and the cycles of nature, which have no meaning apart from time, there stands the biblical notion of the kingdom of God. God's kingdom is not given primary significance by concepts of past, present, and future but rather through *imminence*. God's reign is not timeless, in the sense that it always was and always will be. It is free from the strictures of time in that at any moment it may appear, like a master coming home from a wedding feast at an hour that his servants cannot know.

It is this notion of God's reign as imminent, just over the horizon, always about to appear, that made the watchman such a potent symbol for Israel. In ancient times the fortified cities of the Middle East had watchmen posted in towers upon the walls, ever vigilant for the first sign of an advancing enemy army. The prophets, who watched for signs of God's appearing, were called watchmen. God says to Ezekiel, "So you, son of man, I have made a watchman for the house of Israel; whenever you hear a word from my mouth, you shall give them warning from me" (Ezek. 33:7). By inference, Israel was to be God's watchman for the nations, to give warning that the Day of the Lord was at hand. It is in this sense that another prophet could speak of Israel as "a light to the nations" (Isa. 42:6).

In the New Testament the metaphor of watchman is transformed into that of wakefulness. Paul wrote to the Christians in Rome, "It is full time now for you to wake from sleep" (Rom. 13:11). He cautioned the church in Thessalonica, "So then let us not sleep, as others do, but let us keep awake and be sober" (1 Thess. 5:6).

The faithful of God are those who keep awake, who watch for any sign of the advent of the kingdom. God's reign comes not at the end of an inclined plane, or as the climax of class struggle, or with the turning of the nature cycles, or in the form of an earthly empire—Pax Romana or Pax Americana—but like a thief in the night! The Gospel commentary on Jesus' Parable of the Watchful Servants, as we have seen, is: "But know this, that if the householder had known at what hour the thief was coming, he would not have left his house to be broken into."

Even so, the Christian church is to be like the watchful servants in the parable—never lulled to sleep by any delay in the Master's coming, but ever awake and watchful and ready to open to him when he comes. The writer of the book of Revelation gave to the church in Sardis this charge:

> Awake, and strengthen what remains and is on the point of death, for I have not found your works perfect in the sight of my God. Remember then what you received and heard; keep that, and repent. If you will not awake, I will come like a thief, and you will not know at what hour I will come upon you.
>
> (Revelation 3:2–3)

So strictly are our lives ruled by clocks and calendars that we may find these New Testament warnings arcane. After all, to be human means to be time-bound. One of the greatest of cultural achievements was the invention of the notion of time. How can we imagine human beings apart from some notion of time? Without time, all the technical marvels of our generation would be impossible. Space travel depends upon the precise time that computers measure. But we need to remember that time is a human construct. God's realm is not like our kingdoms; it does not operate by clocks, computers, or calendars. Therefore God's kingdom may come upon us like a thief in the night, or like a master suddenly returning from a wedding feast and knocking on the door for admittance. The faithful are those who are wakeful and watchful.

Work and Sleep

The metaphor of wakeful watching is apt for the contemporary workplace. Anyone who has a job will recognize and heed the warning to keep awake and on the
watch. In both a figurative and literal sense, sleep is the
enemy of work. The locomotive engineer who falls asleep
at the throttle may miss a warning signal and hit another
train. Housekeepers who sleep late find that the housework gets ahead of them. The student who falls asleep in
the midst of the exam is likely to flunk the course.

Sleep is the enemy of work in a figurative as well as a
literal sense. Workers who become so routinized that
they fail to be aware of new possibilities prove ineffective. In the Three Mile Island nuclear disaster, engineers
at the plant saw warning lights but disregarded them.
They might as well have had their heads on their arms,
snoozing away the hours, while the trouble in the reactor
developed into a near catastrophe.

Though sleep is work's enemy, work itself has a curious
way of putting us to sleep. Labor is exhausting; near the
end of the day the temptation is often overpowering to
put the head down on the desk to catch a few winks. It is
not surprising that transcontinental drivers of heavy
trucks sometimes fall asleep and plunge their rigs off the
road. They may have been driving too far with too little
rest.

The classic illustration of the figurative sense in which
work puts people to sleep is Pearl Harbor, December 7,
1941. It was an ideal time for a sneak attack: Sunday
morning, the traditional day of rest, when folk were least
likely to be alert to the new, the sudden, the unexpected.
Those on watch saw signs of an approaching air armada

but disregarded them. They might as well have been tucked up in bed with the covers over their heads. Work has a way of making us deaf and blind to the novel, the unexpected—even to the threatening.

Awake to the Kingdom

Jesus' Parable of the Watchful Servants is not simply a piece of worldly wisdom about not falling asleep on the job. We have not understood the other parables as simple moralisms; we want to avoid any such interpretation of this parable. How, then, can the Parable of the Watchful Servants become a model for those of us who would be faithful to Christ in the workplace?

Certainly it cannot mean for us simply, "Do not fall asleep on the job." We don't need Jesus to remind us of that. From childhood on we have known the fable of the ant and the grasshopper: the hardworking ant, who knew that winter was near and slaved to prepare for it, while the lazy, carefree grasshopper wasted away the sunlit hours and when winter came was literally "out in the cold." Nature itself teaches us the folly of laziness.

Nor do we need Jesus to remind us to keep our minds on what we do at work. When we were children, we were told the legend of King Alfred of England, who stopped one day—unrecognized—at the home of a cottager. She gave him a seat by the fire and set him to watch some cakes that were browning. The good king got to mulling over the problems of his kingdom and let the cakes burn. We've known a hundred King Alfreds; we don't need Jesus to warn us to keep our minds on our work.

If the parable cannot mean any of the above, what can it mean? Read in the context of our daily work, with our natural tendencies to fall asleep, the meaning of the parable is this: *God's kingdom is at the door. We are not to allow our work so to dull our minds that we cannot see the possibilities of that kingdom being revealed even today.*

The present time is pregnant with the possibility that God's kingdom may be seen and heard among us. We may work as those who are awake to the imminent possibility of its appearing.

Paulo Freire is a Brazilian educator, known for his work among the illiterate peasants of his country. He found them to be singularly lacking in any sense of self-worth. Years of illiteracy and oppression had made them almost zombies. When he had taught them to read and to look at themselves as those with the power to make their world different, how things changed! In one of his books, Freire quotes an elderly peasant as saying that he now knows himself to be cultured. And when Freire asks him how he knows this, the man replies, "I work, and in working I transform the world." Such a person, waked from sleep, is not far from the kingdom of God.

CHRISTIAN HERALD ASSOCIATION AND ITS MINISTRIES

CHRISTIAN HERALD ASSOCIATION, founded in 1878, publishes The Christian Herald Magazine, one of the leading interdenominational religious monthlies in America. Through its wide circulation, it brings inspiring articles and the latest news of religious developments to many families. From the magazine's pages came the initiative for CHRISTIAN HERALD CHILDREN and THE BOWERY MISSION, two individually supported not-for-profit corporations.

CHRISTIAN HERALD CHILDREN, established in 1894, is the name for a unique and dynamic ministry to disadvantaged children, offering hope and opportunities which would not otherwise be available for reasons of poverty and neglect. The goal is to develop each child's potential and to demonstrate Christian compassion and understanding to children in need.

Mont Lawn is a permanent camp located in Bushkill, Pennsylvania. It is the focal point of a ministry which provides a healthful "vacation with a purpose" to children who without it would be confined to the streets of the city. Up to 1000 children between the age of 7 and 11 come to Mont Lawn each year.

Christian Herald Children maintains year-round contact with children by means of a *City Youth Ministry.* Central to its philosophy is the belief that only through sustained relationships and demonstrated concern can individual lives be truly enriched. Special emphasis is on individual guidance, spiritual and family counseling and tutoring. This follow-up ministry to inner-city children culminates for many in financial assistance toward higher education and career counseling.

THE BOWERY MISSION, located at 227 Bowery, New York City, has since 1879 been reaching out to the lost men on the Bowery, offering them what could be their last chance to rebuild their lives. Every man is fed, clothed and ministered to. Countless numbers have entered the 90-day residential rehabilitation program at the Bowery Mission. A concentrated ministry of counseling, medical care, nutrition therapy, Bible study and Gospel services awakens a man to spiritual renewal within himself.

These ministries are supported solely by the voluntary contributions of individuals and by legacies and bequests. Contributions are tax deductible. Checks should be made out either to CHRISTIAN HERALD CHILDREN or to THE BOWERY MISSION.

Administrative Office: 40 Overlook Drive, Chappaqua, New York 10514
Telephone: (914) 769-9000